JCL CENTRE FOR HOLOCAUST EDUCATION

UNDERSTANDING THE HOLOCAUST

How and why did it happen?

KS3

Stuart Foster ● Andy Pearce
Eleni Karayianni ● Helen McCord

Many people have contributed to the development and production of this textbook. In particular we would like to thank the following for their support and expertise: Roxzann Baker, Ben Barkow, Shoshana Boyd Gelfand, Amy Braier, Beth Cleall, Mary Fulbrook, Evangelos Himonides, Charlotte Lane, Tom Lawson, Trevor Pears, Josie Roberts, Paul Salmons, Toby Simpson, Dan Stone, Kirsty Taylor, Euan Wallace and Barbara Warnock.

We would also like to thank our colleagues at the UCL Centre for Holocaust Education for their support and educational input: Arthur Chapman, Andrew Copeland, Rebecca Hale, Tom Haward, Emma O'Brien, Jeff Marks, Louise Palmer, Alice Pettigrew, Corey Soper, Shazia Syed and Nicola Wetherall.

We are particularly grateful to Ruth-Anne Lenga, Programme Director, for her support in the development of the pages focused on Holocaust survivors in Great Britain.

The University College London (UCL) Centre for Holocaust Education is part of the UCL Institute of Education – currently the world's leading university for education – and comprises a team of specialist researchers and educators. Its mission is to offer world-class, research-informed support to teachers who teach about the Holocaust and to significantly improve students' knowledge and understanding of this history and its contemporary significance. On an annual basis approximately 2,000 teachers participate in the Centre's programmes.

All four authors work at the Centre. Professor Stuart Foster is Executive Director; Dr. Andy Pearce is Associate Professor in History and Holocaust Education; Dr. Eleni Karayianni is a Research Fellow; and Helen McCord is a Senior Teaching Fellow.

HODDER EDUCATION

AN HACHETTE UK COMPANY

The Publishers would like to thank the following for permission to reproduce copyright material.

Photo credits

p.6 Yad Vashem Hall of Names Dep.; p.11 *1st row: l* United States Holocaust Memorial Museum (USHMM), courtesy of The Shtetl Foundation; *lc* USHMM, courtesy of Archiwum Panstwowe w Rzeszow; *rc* Bildarchiv Pisarek/akg-images; *r* USHMM, courtesy of Henry Kopelman-Gidoni; *2nd row: l* USHMM, courtesy of Jack Beraha; *lc* USHMM, courtesy of Leon Rozenbaum; *rc* USHMM, courtesy of Norman Salsitz; *r* USHMM, courtesy of Malvina Burstein; *3rd row: l* USHMM, courtesy of Jack Beraha; *lc* USHMM, courtesy of Marilka (Mairanz) Ben Naim, Ita (Mairanz) Mond and Tuvia Mairanz; *rc* USHMM, courtesy of The Shtetl Foundation; *r* USHMM, courtesy of Association for the Lithuanian Jews in Israel; *4th row: l* USHMM, courtesy of Jacqueline Gal; *c* USHMM, courtesy of Gabriel Albocher; *r* USHMM, courtesy of Robert Bahr; p.12 © Josef Mendelsohn; *r* Holocaust Center for Humanity; p.13 © The Jewish Museum via Getty Images; p.14 © MARTYN HAYHOW/AFP via Getty Images; *l* © Lebrecht Music / Alamy Stock Photo; *r* USHMM, courtesy of Frances Hirshfeld; p.15 *t* USHMM, courtesy of Richard Oestermann; *b* USHMM, courtesy of George Fogelson; p.17 © British Library Board. All Rights Reserved/Bridgeman Images; p.18 *tl* Wiener Holocaust Library Collections; *bl* © Apic/Getty Images; *tr* Library of Congress Prints & Photographs Division, LC-USZ62-60242; *cr* Public domain: Photo: Fotograaf Onbekend/Anefo/National Archives of the Netherlands; *br* © History and Art Collection/Alamy Stock Photo; p.22 *r* © Everett Collection Inc/Alamy Stock Photo; p.23 *t & l* © Bundesarchiv; *r* © INTERFOTO/Alamy Stock Photo; p.24 *t & b* © Bundesarchiv; p.25 Wiener Holocaust Library Collections; p.26 *l & r* © Sueddeutsche Zeitung Photo/Alamy Stock Photo; p.27 Dachau Memorial site (KZ-Gedenkstätte Dachau), Da A F9/8405; p.28 *l* NS-Documentation Center of the City of Cologne; p.29 *t* © dpa picture alliance/Alamy Stock Photo; p.30 USHMM, courtesy of Waltraud & Annemarie Kusserow; p.31 *l* USHMM; *r* Jean-Luc SCHWAB /https://commons.wikimedia.org/wiki/File:Rudolf_BRAZDA_-_April_15th_2009.jpg/ https://creativecommons.org/licenses/by-sa/3.0/deed.en; *b* Wiener Holocaust Library Collections; p.32 *l* © Marianne Bechhaus-Gerst; *r* © Bianca Stojka Davis; *b* © Sigrid Falkenstein; p.34 *t* © Sueddeutsche Zeitung Photo/Alamy Stock Photo; *b* USHMM, courtesy of National Archives and Records Administration, College Park; p.36–7 *all* Wiener Holocaust Library Collections; p.40 © World History Archive/Alamy Stock Photo; p.41 *l* USHMM, courtesy of National Archives and Records Administration, College Park; *r* Universalmuseum Joanneum GmbH; p.42 American Jewish Joint Distribution Committee; p.46 © TopFoto/Alamy Stock Photo; p.48 *l* Wiener Holocaust Library Collections; *r* Yad Vashem Photo Archive, Jerusalem; p.49 From the Archives of the YIVO Institute for Jewish Research, New York; p.50 Northcliffe Collection/ANL/Shutterstock; p.53 RIA Novosti / Sputnik / TopFoto; p.54 Archives of the Hamburg Institute for Social Research; p.55 © The History Collection / Alamy Stock Photo; *r* National Digital Archives of Poland (Narodowe Archiwum Cyfrowe) /Collection Koncern Ilustrowany Kurier Codzienny – Archiwum Ilustracji; p.56 /USHMM/Ernst Klee Archive; p.57 © Everett Collection Inc / Alamy Stock Photo; p.60 © The Picture Art Collection / Alamy Stock Photo; p.61–2 *t* Archive of the Auschwitz-Birkenau State Museum; p.62 *b* Yad Vashem Photo Archive, Jerusalem 5683719; p.63 akg-images / Benno Gantner; *r* © www.auschwitz.org; *c* © Imperial War Museum (IWM FLM 1226); *b* © Horace Abrahams/Keystone/Getty Images; p.67 *bl* USHMM, courtesy of Eliezer Zilberis; *cr* Yad Vashem Photo Archive, Jerusalem 37GO4; *br* USHMM, courtesy of Leopold Page Photographic Collection; p.68 *t* Yad Vashem Photo Archive, Jerusalem 39262; *c & b* E. Ringelblum Jewish Historical Institute, Warsaw, Poland; p.70 US National Archives and Records Administration, 238-NT-282; p.71 / Ghetto Fighters' House, Israel, photo archive; *r* Yad Vashem Photo Archive, Jerusalem 4613/664; p.72 © Bundesarchiv; p.73 *l* USHMM, courtesy of Saulius Berzinis; *r* USHMM, courtesy of Instytut Pamieci Narodowej; *b* © Bundesarchiv; p.74 *l* US National Archives; *r* © Sueddeutsche Zeitung Photo / Alamy Stock Photo; *b* USHMM, courtesy of Michael O'Hara; p.75 *l* Bildarchiv Preussischer Kulturbesitz; *b* © United Archives GmbH / Alamy Stock Photo; p.77 *t & b* The Museum of Danish Resistance 1940-1945; p.78 Righteous Collection, Yad Vashem; p.79 *l & r* Yad Vashem Photo Archive, Jerusalem 28163 (*l*) and 26621 (*r*); p.82 *l* USHMM, courtesy of National Archives and Records Administration, College Park; *r* The Bernard Simon Estate, Wiener Holocaust Library Collections; *b* USHMM, courtesy of Erica & Joseph Grossman; p.83 *l* © Crown copyright 2015; *r* © Leicester University Press, used by permission of Bloomsbury Publishing Plc; *b* Tzahy Lerner/ https://commons.wikimedia.org/wiki/ File:Yehuda_Bauer_1.jpg; p.85 *l* Yad Vashem Photo Archive, Jerusalem 3488/18; *c* Christian Herrmann; *r* © John Warburton-Lee Photography / Alamy Stock Photo; p.87 Yad Vashem Photo Archive, Jerusalem FA180/46; p.88 USHMM, courtesy of Willy Fogel; p.89 *t* USHMM, courtesy of Nordico Museum Der Stadt Linz; *b* USHMM, courtesy of Bernard Marks; p.91 © Ian Waldie/Getty Images; p.92 © Volgi archive / Alamy Stock Photo; p.93 © Bettmann/Getty Images.

Text credits

p.13 'Glimpses of life before the Holocaust', Yad Vashem; p.14 & 15 British Library Sound Archive; p.19 *t & b* 'Why did people hate us?', Imperial War Museum; p.28 *t* Melita Maschmann, *Account Rendered: A Dossier on my Former Self*; p.36 *t* 'From Citizens to Outcasts', USHMM; *b* 'Jewish life in Germany', Yad Vashem; p.41 *t* '*Kristallnacht* in a small German town', Yad Vashem; *b* Wiener Library; p.48 *t* 'Everyday life in a Warsaw Ghetto', Yad Vashem; *b* Diary of Pepa Bergman, Yad Vashem; p.57 'Chelmno – A Testimony', Yad Vashem; p.64 *l & r* 'The Death Marches January–May 1945', Yehuda Bauer, Modern Judaism – A Journal of Jewish Ideas and Experience, 3, 1, 1983'; p.77 'The Holocaust and Collective Memory in Scandinavia: the Danish case', Karl Christian Lammers, Scandinavian Journal of History, 36, 5, 2011; p.78 Norman H. Gershman, *Besa: Muslims Who Saved Jews During WWII*; p.87 Yitzchak Zuckerman *The Exodus from Poland*, Ghetto Fighters' House; p.91 *r* © Leon Greenman, used by permission of Ruth-Anne Lenga; p.93 Mary Fulbrook, *Reckonings: Legacies of Nazi Persecution and the Quest for Justice*.

Acknowledgements

Every effort has been made to trace all copyright holders, but if any have been inadvertently overlooked, the Publishers will be pleased to make the necessary arrangements at the first opportunity.

Although every effort has been made to ensure that website addresses are correct at time of going to press, Hodder Education cannot be held responsible for the content of any website mentioned in this book. It is sometimes possible to find a relocated web page by typing in the address of the home page for a website in the URL window of your browser.

Hachette UK's policy is to use papers that are natural, renewable and recyclable products and made from wood grown in well-managed forests and other controlled sources. The logging and manufacturing processes are expected to conform to the environmental regulations of the country of origin.

Orders: please contact Bookpoint Ltd, 130 Park Drive, Milton Park, Abingdon, Oxon OX14 4SE. Telephone: +44 (0)1235 827827. Fax: +44 (0)1235 400401. Email education@bookpoint.co.uk Lines are open from 9 a.m. to 5 p.m., Monday to Saturday, with a 24-hour message answering service. You can also order through our website: www.hoddereducation.co.uk

ISBN: 978 1 5104 8037 7

Cover photo from the United States Holocaust Memorial Museum, courtesy of George Pick

Illustrations by Chris Bladon Design

Typeset in the United Kingdom

Printed in the United Kingdom

A catalogue record for this title is available from the British Library.

MIX
Paper from responsible sources
FSC™ C104740
www.fsc.org

Contents

This textbook is divided into six units. Each of these units contain chapters. Every unit covers a specific time period and has an overall theme. Units begin with a one-page overview. This overview outlines:

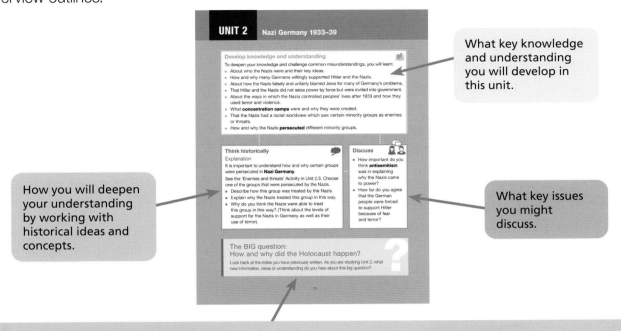

What key knowledge and understanding you will develop in this unit.

How you will deepen your understanding by working with historical ideas and concepts.

What key issues you might discuss.

How and why did the Holocaust happen?

These two very important questions are not the same, but they are closely related. This textbook is designed to help you answer both questions. It does so by treating them as 'the BIG question'. As you move through each chapter and unit, you will build up your knowledge and understanding of the Holocaust. This will enable you to answer 'the BIG question' of how and why in more detailed and more powerful ways. Remember to come back to 'the BIG question' at the end of each unit.

Chapters

Each chapter is focused on a particular enquiry question, and contains the information you need to explore and answer this question. Also included in the chapters are 'Think about' boxes and 'Activities'. These are focused on what you have been learning about in a chapter. They help reinforce what you know, deepen what you understand, and support you as you reflect on your learning.

Online knowledge checks

Throughout the book, you will find pointers to go online in order to check your own knowledge. Visit the UCL Centre for Holocaust Education website where you can take short quizzes.

Key words

You will see these in the text as they will be in **bold**. To find out what these words mean, use the Glossary at the back of the book.

The Pitel family

Look carefully at the 26 people in Figure 0.1. The photograph shows the members of a large Jewish family who lived in a small town in Eastern Poland. It was taken in 1938, one year before the Second World War began. Think about the lives these people might have lived, the hopes and dreams they may have had for the future.

Incredibly, just five years later, every person in this photograph, except for one, had been murdered.

The only person who survived beyond 1943 was Yosef Pitel (the man on the far right). He survived because soon after this photograph was taken, he left Poland to begin a new life more than a thousand miles away in a country which is now known as **Israel**.

In 1938, he had no idea just how precious this photograph would become – and that he would never see any of his family again.

Figure 0.1 The Pitel family

The fate of the Pitel family

In September 1939, **Nazi Germany** invaded Poland. By 1943 all of the Pitel family, apart from Yosef, were killed. Some died in **ghettos**, others were murdered by gassing in a Nazi **death camp**. Millions of other innocent people just like them were murdered because they were Jewish. This mass killing is known as the Holocaust.

In this book you will learn about the Holocaust and how and why the Pitel family and millions of other victims were killed by the Nazis and their **collaborators**.

What was the Holocaust?

Adolf Hitler and the Nazis came to power in Germany in 1933. Between 1933 and 1939, Jews in Germany faced terrible **discrimination** and **prejudice** and some were killed. However, it was during the Second World War (1939–1945) that the mass killing of approximately six million Jews across Europe occurred.

The Nazis and their collaborators wanted to totally destroy Jewish life in Europe. Jewish people were victims of **genocide**. Genocide is any act committed with intent to destroy, in whole or in part, a national, ethnic, racial or religious group. The defeat of Nazi Germany and its **allies** in 1945 brought the killings to an end. However, by this time two-thirds of Jews who lived in Europe before the war were killed, including approximately 90 per cent of all Jewish children. If you look closely at the map on pages 8–9 you can see the scale of the murder in countries all over Europe.

Persecution, murder, genocide

During this period the **Roma and Sinti** people (sometimes called 'Gypsies') also faced terrible discrimination, brutal treatment, and imprisonment in Nazi camps. An estimated 500,000 were murdered during the Second World War. The Roma and Sinti people were victims of genocide.

Many other groups were also victims of the Nazis and their collaborators. These included disabled people, gay men, **Jehovah's Witnesses**, **political opponents**, Polish and Soviet civilians, and prisoners of war from the Soviet Union.

The BIG question:
How and why did the Holocaust happen?

Before you begin the first unit, note down any ideas you have about how and why the Holocaust happened.

Country	Jewish population c.1933 in countries later controlled or occupied by the Nazis
Albania	200
Austria	191,000
Belgium	60,000
Bulgaria	48,500
Czechoslovakia	357,000
Denmark	5,700
Estonia	4,560
Finland	1,800
France	250,000
Germany	525,000
Greece	73,000
Hungary	445,000
Italy	48,000
Latvia	95,600
Lithuania	155,000
Luxembourg	2,200
Netherlands	156,000
Norway	1,400
Poland	3,000,000
Romania	756,000
Soviet Union	2,525,000
Yugoslavia	68,000

Country	Jewish population c.1933 in countries not occupied by the Nazis
Great Britain	300,000
Ireland	3,600
Portugal	1,200
Spain	4,000
Sweden	6,700
Switzerland	18,000

Figure 0.2 The number of Jewish people murdered in the Holocaust, by country.

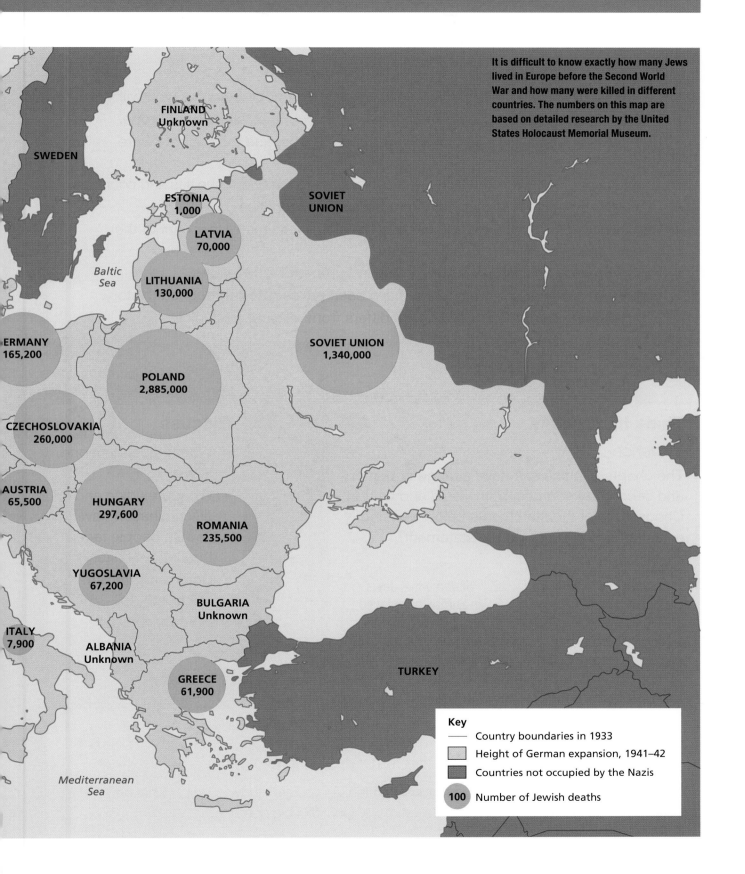

It is difficult to know exactly how many Jews lived in Europe before the Second World War and how many were killed in different countries. The numbers on this map are based on detailed research by the United States Holocaust Memorial Museum.

FINLAND
Unknown

SWEDEN

ESTONIA
1,000

SOVIET
UNION

LATVIA
70,000

Baltic
Sea

LITHUANIA
130,000

SOVIET UNION
1,340,000

ERMANY
165,200

POLAND
2,885,000

CZECHOSLOVAKIA
260,000

AUSTRIA
65,500

HUNGARY
297,600

ROMANIA
235,500

YUGOSLAVIA
67,200

BULGARIA
Unknown

ITALY
7,900

ALBANIA
Unknown

GREECE
61,900

TURKEY

Mediterranean
Sea

Key
—— Country boundaries in 1933
▢ Height of German expansion, 1941–42
▢ Countries not occupied by the Nazis
● 100 Number of Jewish deaths

Develop knowledge and understanding

To deepen your knowledge and challenge common misunderstandings, you will learn:

- That before the Holocaust Jewish people lived in countries all across Europe.
- That Jewish people were employed in all types of jobs, and the majority were not wealthy.
- About some of the ways in which Jews contributed to their communities and countries.
- That Jewish people had many different beliefs and identities.
- That Jews in Germany were a very small minority – less than 1 per cent of the German population.
- That **prejudice** against Jews has existed in Europe for 2,000 years.
- About the many ways in which Jews have been **persecuted** throughout history.
- What **antisemitism** means and how it differs from religious prejudice.

Think historically

Evidence

The chapters in this unit have a range of primary and secondary sources, both visual and written. Choose one of the statements below and find evidence which supports the statement.

Statement 1: Jewish life in Europe before the Second World War was diverse.

Statement 2: Jews in Europe have faced prejudice across time.

Discuss

- What made someone Jewish?
- What prejudice and discrimination have Jewish people faced throughout history?
- Does antisemitism still exist?

The BIG question:
How and why did the Holocaust happen?

Look back at the notes you have previously written. As you are studying Unit 1, what new information, ideas or understanding do you have about this big question?

1.1 Who were the Jews of Europe before the Second World War?

Activities

1 Look at the photographs on this page. What do these images tell us about Jewish people who lived in Europe before the Second World War?

2 On the next two pages, you will read about four individuals: Julius, Laura, Leon and Esther. Look back at the map on pages 8–9 and find the countries where they lived.

3 What can we learn about 'Jewish identity' from these individual case studies?

Jewish people across Europe

FACTS AND STATISTICS

Jews in Europe in 1933

- In 1933, 9.5 million Jews lived in Europe.

- Jewish people had lived in Europe for over 2,000 years.

- There were Jewish communities in every European country.

- More Jews lived in the east than in the west of Europe. Most lived in Poland, the Soviet Union and Romania.

- The majority of Jewish people were not wealthy.

- Many worked in trade and commerce, but Jewish people did all sorts of jobs.

- Not all Jews were religious, and religious Jews did not all believe the same thing.

- The majority were very passionate about the country in which they lived.

Julius Paltiel

Julius was born in Trondheim, Norway, in 1924. His grandfather had settled in Norway in the 1880s. When Julius was growing up there were around 250 Jews living in the city of Trondheim.

Julius's parents ran a clothes store and the family lived above the shop. He had a very happy childhood. He loved sports and, when he was 15, Julius became a manager in the family shop.

Laura Varon

Photo credit: Holocaust Center for Humanity

Laura was born in 1926. Before the Second World War, Laura lived with her family on the Greek island of Rhodes. Her father's family came from Turkey and her mother's from Spain. Jews had lived on the island for over 2,000 years. In the 1930s, around a quarter of the island's population were Jewish.

Laura's family were **Orthodox Jews**. They took part in particular rituals and customs. Laura loved spending Saturday evenings listening to her father telling stories.

Leon Greenman

Leon was born in Stepney Green, London, in 1910. His mother, who died when Leon was two years old, came from a family of Russian Jews. His father's parents came from Rotterdam in the Netherlands. Leon spent much of his childhood in the Netherlands.

In the 1920s, Leon returned to London and trained as a hairdresser. He was not religious and preferred to spend his time boxing and singing. Leon married Else, in 1935. They decided to live in Rotterdam.

Esther Brunstein

Born in 1928, Esther lived in Łódź, Poland. Łódź was a large industrial city, and about one-third of the population was Jewish.

Esther's father worked as a weaver in a factory. Both her parents were active in politics. They were members of the *Bund* – a political movement particularly concerned with the lives of workers. Esther's home was a happy one, and she was influenced by her parents' beliefs and her schooling. She had a strong sense of being both Jewish and Polish.

Jews in Europe before the Second World War

Europe has been home to Jewish people for over 2,000 years. Throughout this time, Jews made a huge contribution to the countries and communities in which they lived.

The way Jews lived before the outbreak of the Second World War and the way they saw the world varied from place to place. For many Jewish people in Europe, being Jewish was not the only part of their identity. A Jewish person could have lots of different ideas, interests and beliefs – just like everyone else. And what a Jewish person thought or believed could change over time. For instance, from the eighteenth century, national identity (such as being British, or French, or German) became

very important to many Jews. You can learn about the experiences of Jewish people on the pages that follow.

Source 1.1

There was no one way to be a Jew, they were traditional and modern, and orthodox and progressive and every shade in between. They were Nobel Prize winners and they were tailors and tradesmen. They were wealthy and they were so poor they couldn't afford shoes for their children in the winter. They went to religious schools, they prayed, and they respected the 2,000-year-old Jewish tradition. But they also went to the movies, played sports and danced the tango. They fell in love, had fun. They were busy with life, looking toward the future.

Sheryl Silver Ochayon, Holocaust educator

Ways of life in Eastern Europe

In parts of Eastern Europe at the beginning of the twentieth century, a growing number of Jews moved to large towns and cities. For example, 350,000 Jews lived in Warsaw (Poland) before the Second World War, 200,000 lived in Budapest (Hungary) and 140,500 lived in Kiev (Ukraine). However, for millions of Jews, life was much the same as it had been for the previous hundred years. Most Jews still lived in **shtetls**. Life in *shtetls* tended to be traditional: people spoke **Yiddish** and religious practices and cultural customs were very important. Within a *shtetl*, people did all sorts of jobs. While some were more comfortably off than others, most were poor and life was hard.

Source 1.2

I was born in 1930 in Ukraine. We were a very religious community. Every morning at 6 o'clock I had to go to the synagogue. Then the Cheder [religious school] from 6 to 8. From 8 o'clock to 4, I went to the state school. [Then] go to Cheder from say about half past 4, till afternoon prayers. Go home and have a meal and then go back to Cheder till 9 or half past 9 in the evening. And that went [on] through summer and winter.

From the testimony of Josef Perl

Figure 1.1 Chelm, a Jewish *shtetl*, Eastern Poland, c.1916–18.

Figure 1.2 A Jewish family strolls along a street in Kalisz, Poland, 16 May 1935.

Ways of life in Western Europe

Jewish life in Western Europe was often different. For example, *shtetls* did not exist in these countries. In places such as Britain, France and Germany, the majority of Jews lived alongside non-Jews in large towns and cities. Partly because of this, Jewish communities in the west were often less traditional than those in the east.

Source 1.3

I was born in a Parisian suburb, in 1910. My father was a teacher in the [high school]. We lived in a non-Jewish community … My grandfather – my father's father – was not religious at all. My mother's parents, especially her mother, were extremely religious. I was conscious of my Jewishness because my grandmother was such a devout religious woman. [When she came to stay] it was a bit difficult because my father didn't want the religion to interfere with our daily life. We had of course to change the menu [what we ate]. And wait until she had finished her prayers, but that was all.

From the testimony of Claudette Kennedy

Figure 1.3 The Oestermann children relax on a beach in Denmark, 1936.

The Jews of Germany

In a country of 67 million people, German Jews were a very small minority. They made up less than 1 per cent of the population – just 525,000 people. Over previous centuries, many Jews had moved to Germany, partly to escape prejudice and persecution elsewhere. By the 1930s, Jewish people in Germany were very **assimilated**.

The majority of Jews saw themselves as Germans and were proud of it. In fact, approximately 100,000 German Jewish men served in the German army during the First World War. Around 12,000 were killed in action and 30,000 were decorated for their bravery.

Although religion was still important to many Jews, large numbers were either not religious or had less traditional beliefs. While some Jewish people still lived in towns and villages, most made their homes in cities. These men and women did various jobs. Many were teachers, doctors, or worked in the arts or in business.

Figure 1.4 Three Jewish sisters sledging in the Berlin Tiergarten, 1929.

Think about

How did 'Jewish identities' differ from each other?

1.2 What prejudice did Jews face?

Life for Jews was not always easy. For long periods of time, Jewish people across Europe were treated differently by their non-Jewish neighbours. Sometimes there were even violent attacks on Jews.

The reasons for this hostility are complicated and go back 2,000 years to Roman times. The relationship between Jews and Romans changed as the Roman Empire grew. When Christianity became the official religion of the Empire in the fourth century, Judaism became a rival religion, and some early Christians wrongly claimed that Jews had killed Jesus.

By the year 1000 CE, almost everyone in Europe was Christian. Jews, who did not share Christian beliefs, became the target for brutal persecution. Lies about Jews spread and Jews became **demonised** and wrongly blamed for crises such as plagues. They became a **scapegoat** for people's problems.

The rulers of different countries passed laws that were unfair towards Jews. This included stopping Jewish people from doing certain jobs, or making them live separately from non-Jews in **ghettos**. Jews were often forced to wear hats, badges or certain items of clothing to show they were Jewish.

On numerous occasions throughout history, Jews were forced to leave their country. Every time they were **expelled**, they had to find another place to settle. This caused great movement of Jewish **refugees** across Europe and beyond. With the spread of Christianity across the world, it was difficult for Jews to find a welcoming place to live.

Jewish life in Medieval England

We do not know when Jewish people first came to England. However, after he became King in 1066, William the Conqueror encouraged Jews to settle in the country. Jewish people were given protection by the King.

In the 1100s, life for Jews in England changed. Jewish people started to be wrongly accused of murdering Christian children, and anti-Jewish feeling grew.

Violence against Jews spread across the country. One of the worst instances was in York in 1190, when around 150 Jewish people died after being trapped in a tower.

For the next 100 years the Jews of England suffered increasing persecution. Finally, in 1290, King Edward I ordered all Jews to leave the country. England became the first European country to expel Jewish people. It was not until 1655 that these laws were removed and Jews returned.

Figure 1.5 An image of Jews being beaten from a thirteenth-century English manuscript. The figures in blue and yellow are wearing a badge in the shape of two tablets. These represent the Tablets of Stone with the Ten Commandments that Moses received from God in the biblical story (Exodus 20:1–17).

Activities

Undertake your own research to:

1 Find out what happened at York in 1190.

2 Discover how Jewish persecution was linked to the Crusades.

Change across time

As time went by, people's lives began to change. New inventions and discoveries in the seventeenth and eighteenth centuries led people to see the world in different ways and challenge existing ideas. For many, religion was no longer as important as it once was. New attitudes emerged – particularly in Western Europe. Here, more and more people argued that every human being was equal, regardless of their beliefs.

Slowly, many of the laws against Jews began to be lifted. With the ghettos closed and restrictions on jobs lifted, Jews and non-Jews came into even closer contact. As Jewish people took the new opportunities available to them in the eighteenth and nineteenth centuries, they made increasing contributions to the countries in which they lived.

Jewish contributions to European life and culture

During the twentieth century millions of Jews continued to have a positive impact on life and culture in communities across Europe. Here are some examples.

Activity

Choose one of these five people and try to find out more about them.

Albert Einstein

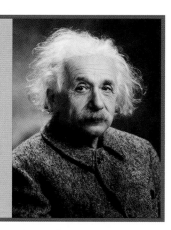

Albert Einstein was born in Germany in 1879. He became a famous physicist whose work completely changed scientific thinking.

Béla Guttmann

Béla Guttmann was a successful football player. He represented Hungary at the Olympics in 1924. As manager of Benfica, he won the European Cup in 1961 and 1962.

Gerty Simon

Gerty Simon was a famous German photographer. She presented her photographs in a number of exhibitions in Berlin during the 1920s and early 1930s.

Janusz Korczak

Janusz Korczak was born in Warsaw, Poland. He was a doctor, an educator and an author. He was one of the first people to speak about the rights of children and he believed that children should be educated with love and respect.

Ida Rubenstein

Ida Rubenstein was born in present-day Ukraine in 1883. She became a famous actor and dancer.

Antisemitism

Hatred of Jews remained. Some Christians continued to have anti-Jewish beliefs. Others, who disliked Jews but were not religious, looked for new ways to justify their beliefs. In 1870, a German politician called Wilhelm Marr introduced a new word to express his beliefs against Jews: 'antisemitism'.

For Marr and his followers, the difference between Jews and non-Jews was not about religion. Instead, they claimed that Jewish people were a different 'race'. Of course, this is not true. However, people who believed in antisemitism did not just think Jews were a different 'race', they also saw Jews as a danger and a threat to the so-called 'Aryan race'.

Antisemitism in Germany

Although antisemitism existed in Germany in 1900, it was not a strong political force. But during and after the First World War, antisemitism grew. Some people claimed that Germany lost the war because of the Jews. This was completely untrue, but played on the long-standing practice of making Jewish people scapegoats.

During the 1920s, antisemitism continued to rise, but German Jews did not feel in great danger. The growing popularity of the Nazis after 1929 was worrying, but even when Hitler became leader of Germany in 1933, many thought he would not be in power long.

Living with antisemitism

Antisemitism could take many different forms but it was always unpleasant and upsetting.

Source 1.4

When I was five years old, my father [a doctor] said … there was a birth of a child during the night, and he was rather worried about this lady and the child, and he wanted to have a look. So we went there, and he left me standing in the courtyard and ... suddenly … children came out from various doors, and eventually they started to call me 'dirty Jewish pig', and they started to throw stones at me. By the time my father came out, I was standing there crying and bleeding.

From the testimony of Trude Levi, Hungary

Source 1.5

Twice a year, … on Easter Friday and Christmas, we had to put up shutters because the windows were smashed because the local priest used to say 'Our Christ who we love has been murdered by the Jews and these Jews live amongst you'.

From the testimony of Roman Halter, Poland

Activities

1 What is antisemitism? Explain antisemitism in your own words.

2 What impact do you think the antisemitic experiences described in Sources 1.4 and 1.5 would have had on Trude and Roman?

3 When and why did prejudice towards Germany's Jews start to change?

Now you have studied this unit, check your knowledge here:
www.ucl.ac.uk/holocaust-education

Develop knowledge and understanding

To deepen your knowledge and challenge common misunderstandings, you will learn:

- About who the Nazis were and their key ideas.
- How and why many Germans willingly supported Hitler and the Nazis.
- About how the Nazis falsely and unfairly blamed Jews for many of Germany's problems.
- That Hitler and the Nazis did not seize power by force but were invited into government.
- About the ways in which the Nazis controlled peoples' lives after 1933 and how they used terror and violence.
- What **concentration camps** were and why they were created.
- That the Nazis had a racist worldview which saw certain minority groups as enemies or threats.
- How and why the Nazis **persecuted** different minority groups.

Think historically

Explanation

It is important to understand how and why certain groups were persecuted in **Nazi Germany**.

See the 'Enemies and threats' Activity in Chapter 2.3. Choose one of the groups that were persecuted by the Nazis.

- Describe how this group was treated by the Nazis.
- Explain why the Nazis treated this group in this way.
- Why do you think the Nazis were able to treat this group in this way? (Think about the levels of support for the Nazis in Germany as well as their use of terror).

Discuss

- How important do you think **propaganda** was in explaining why the Nazis came to power?
- How far do you agree that the German people were forced to support Hitler because of fear and terror?

The BIG question:
How and why did the Holocaust happen?

Look back at the notes you have previously written. As you are studying Unit 2, what new information, ideas or understanding do you have about this big question?

2.1 Who were the Nazis?

After the First World War, life in Germany was very hard, with food shortages and violence on the streets. Many people felt outraged by the Treaty of Versailles (1919). This treaty blamed Germany for the war, gave some former German land to other countries and made Germany pay **compensation**. Like many Germans, Adolf Hitler, a former soldier, was angry and frustrated with Germany's defeat. He had extreme ideas about Germany's future and, in 1919, he joined a small political party. In 1920 they were renamed the National Socialist German Workers Party (NSDAP), known as the Nazi party. In 1921, Hitler became the Nazi party's leader.

Nazi ideas

All political parties have ideas, beliefs and values, which are called an ideology. Ideologies are important because they help to explain the promises politicians make, and what politicians then do when they have power. You can learn more about Nazi ideas and beliefs below.

Think about

In the early years after the First World War, why might Nazi ideas have appealed to some German people?

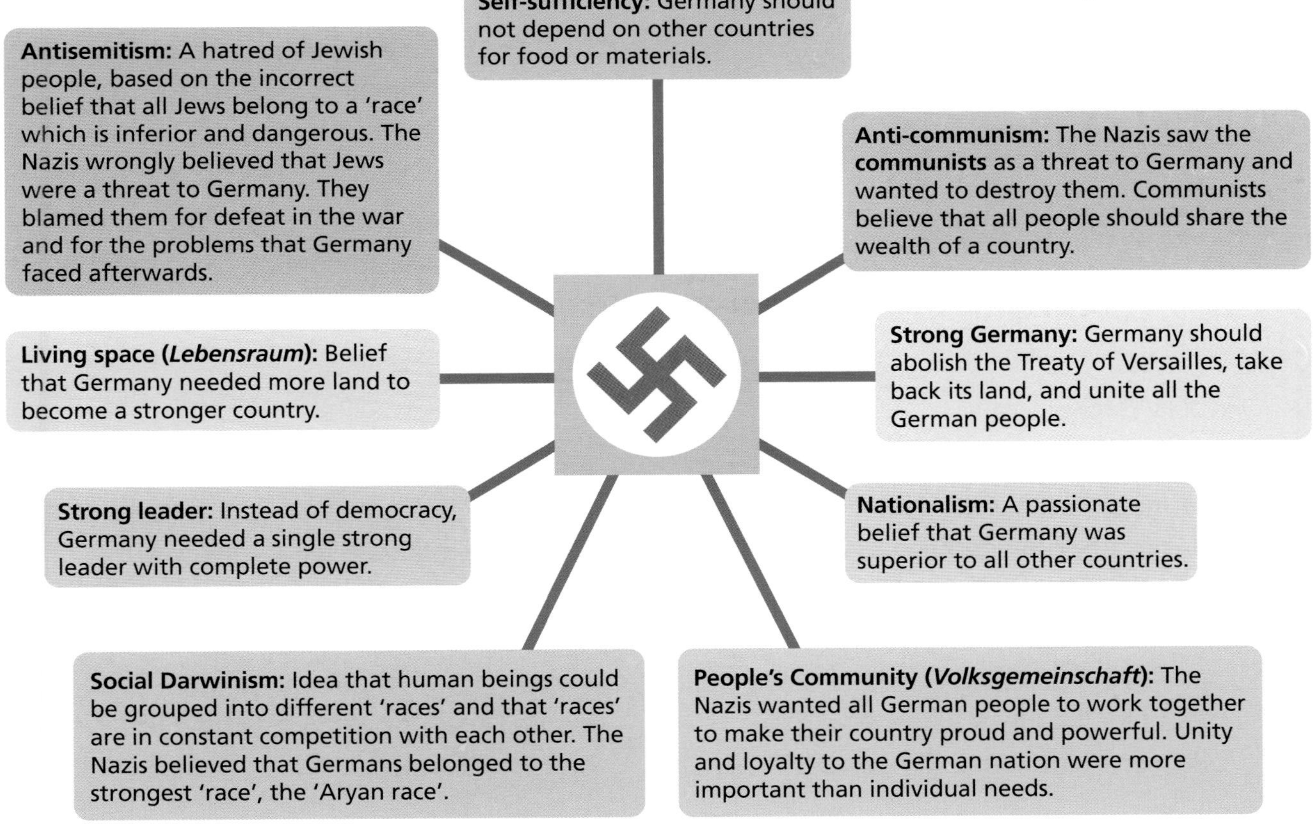

Figure 2.1 Nazi ideas.

Self-sufficiency: Germany should not depend on other countries for food or materials.

Antisemitism: A hatred of Jewish people, based on the incorrect belief that all Jews belong to a 'race' which is inferior and dangerous. The Nazis wrongly believed that Jews were a threat to Germany. They blamed them for defeat in the war and for the problems that Germany faced afterwards.

Anti-communism: The Nazis saw the **communists** as a threat to Germany and wanted to destroy them. Communists believe that all people should share the wealth of a country.

Living space (*Lebensraum*): Belief that Germany needed more land to become a stronger country.

Strong Germany: Germany should abolish the Treaty of Versailles, take back its land, and unite all the German people.

Strong leader: Instead of democracy, Germany needed a single strong leader with complete power.

Nationalism: A passionate belief that Germany was superior to all other countries.

Social Darwinism: Idea that human beings could be grouped into different 'races' and that 'races' are in constant competition with each other. The Nazis believed that Germans belonged to the strongest 'race', the 'Aryan race'.

People's Community (*Volksgemeinschaft*): The Nazis wanted all German people to work together to make their country proud and powerful. Unity and loyalty to the German nation were more important than individual needs.

The rise of the Nazis

Throughout the 1920s, the Nazi party remained small, but from the mid-1920s they were well organised and began to take part in elections. In the 1928 election they only won 2.6 per cent of the vote. Five years later, the Nazis were the largest political party and Hitler was the leader of Germany. How did this happen?

In October 1929, an economic crisis known as 'the **Great Depression**' began. It started in the USA, but spread throughout the world. It seriously affected Germany. Unemployment and homelessness rose and many struggled to feed their families. Hitler and the Nazis offered hope to many Germans. They promised jobs for all Germans, to restore German pride and to get rid of those they claimed were responsible for the chaos. In the July 1932 election, the Nazis won 37 per cent of the vote, making them the largest political party in Germany. Look at Figure 2.2. In the November 1932 election, the number of votes for the Nazis declined. This convinced some, wrongly, that Hitler would therefore be easier to control. On 30 January 1933, Hitler was asked to lead a government.

Figure 2.3 A 1932 election poster: 'Our last hope – Hitler'.

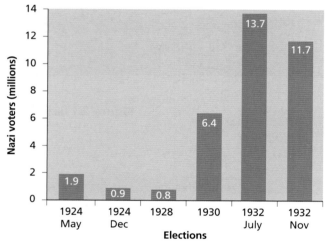

Figure 2.2 The number of people who voted for the Nazi party in elections, 1924–32.

Activities

1 Study Figure 2.2. What happened to the numbers of Germans voting for the Nazi party between the elections of 1928 and 1930?

2 Revisit Figure 2.1, 'Nazi ideas'. Why do you think increasing numbers of Germans voted for the Nazis in the July 1932 election? Nazi ideas remained the same as they had been in the 1920s. So what had changed? Try to explain your answer. Use the poster in Figure 2.3 to help you.

3 The Nazis did not seize power by force, nor did they win enough votes in an election to get them into power. Try to explain in your own words how Hitler became the leader of Germany in 1933.

Why did many Germans vote for Hitler?

Propaganda

In 1930, Joseph Goebbels was put in charge of Nazi **propaganda**. Through newspapers, posters, leaflets, political gatherings and rallies, he was very successful at telling people about Nazi ideas. The Nazis also used 'new' methods (e.g. film, radio, loudspeakers, records) to great effect. Goebbels believed in connecting with people emotionally. At rallies involving massive crowds, the Nazis used torches, music, salutes, flags and songs to bring people together and to create a sense of drama, excitement and belonging.

Joseph Goebbels, head of Nazi propaganda, addresses a massive crowd of supporters, Berlin 1932.

The role of the SA

The SA (*Sturmabteilung*) or Stormtroopers were a group within the Nazi party. They wore military uniforms and would parade, giving the impression of order. The SA were also violent and they would often attack **political opponents** (like communists) in the streets.

Members of the SA parade the streets, making a show of force to intimidate and persuade voters to support Hitler (Spandau, Germany, 1932).

The appeal of Hitler

Nazi propaganda often presented Hitler as the leader and saviour that Germany needed. He was considered to be a great speaker who could connect and excite the crowds. Many Germans believed that Hitler would be a strong leader who could tackle Germany's problems and provide hope for the future.

1932 campaign poster.

Organisation

The party was carefully organised to appeal to all Germans. There were different groups, such as the Hitler Youth, the Nazi Teachers' Association and the Order of German Women. The party also organised local sporting events, fairs and concerts to bring people together in exciting ways. The aim was for people to feel the Nazis were on their side and to create a sense of belonging.

Hitler Youth members give the Nazi salute while riding bikes in Berlin, 1932.

Nazi promises

The Nazis made promises which appealed to different people at a time when many Germans believed that their government had failed to tackle the Great Depression. They promised to protect Germany from the communist 'threat'. This appealed to Germany's business community, who feared that communists would take over their businesses. The Nazis also promised German people jobs, better pensions and support for small businesses and farmers. Unfairly, they blamed Jews for Germany's failures. In times of chaos and difficulty, many Germans were attracted to these ideas.

Members of the SA sit down with a farmer and his wife to try to persuade them to vote for the Nazis, June 1932.

Activities

Historians try to explain what caused events to happen in the past. The information on these pages provides some of the key causes (or explanations) for why Hitler and the Nazis came to power.

1 Identify as many causes as you can that help to explain why many Germans voted for the Nazis.

2 How important do you think antisemitism was in explaining why the Nazis came to power?

2.2 How did the Nazis rule Germany?

Once in power, the Nazis seized opportunities to take control of Germany. In March 1933, the **Enabling Act** was passed, which gave Hitler the sole power to make laws. In July 1933, all other political parties were banned and Germany became a one-party state.

After the death of Germany's president Hindenburg in 1934, Hitler ruled as a **dictator**. As the diagram below shows, the Nazis attempted to control all aspects of people's lives.

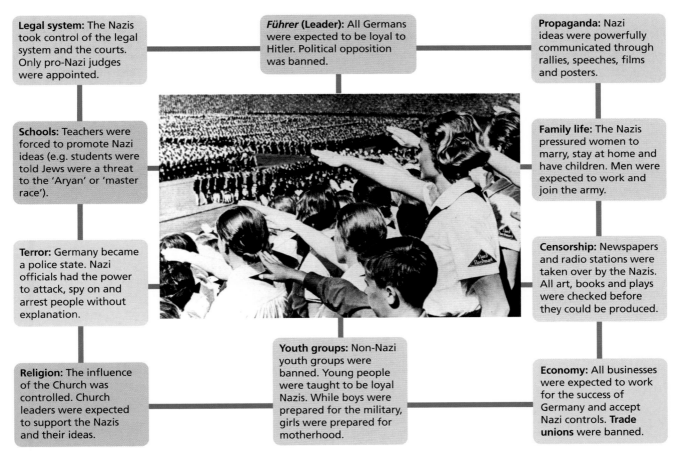

Legal system: The Nazis took control of the legal system and the courts. Only pro-Nazi judges were appointed.

Führer (Leader): All Germans were expected to be loyal to Hitler. Political opposition was banned.

Propaganda: Nazi ideas were powerfully communicated through rallies, speeches, films and posters.

Schools: Teachers were forced to promote Nazi ideas (e.g. students were told Jews were a threat to the 'Aryan' or 'master race').

Family life: The Nazis pressured women to marry, stay at home and have children. Men were expected to work and join the army.

Terror: Germany became a police state. Nazi officials had the power to attack, spy on and arrest people without explanation.

Censorship: Newspapers and radio stations were taken over by the Nazis. All art, books and plays were checked before they could be produced.

Religion: The influence of the Church was controlled. Church leaders were expected to support the Nazis and their ideas.

Youth groups: Non-Nazi youth groups were banned. Young people were taught to be loyal Nazis. While boys were prepared for the military, girls were prepared for motherhood.

Economy: All businesses were expected to work for the success of Germany and accept Nazi controls. **Trade unions** were banned.

Figure 2.4 How the Nazis controlled Germany.

Activity

Pick three of the methods of control in the diagram. Explain how each of these would have helped the Nazis to rule over the German people.

Think about

Why do you think the Nazis were keen to gain the support of young people? How might this have helped them to keep control in Germany?

Violence and the police state

During the 1920s, the Nazis used violence against their opponents (people who disagreed with Nazi ideas). After taking power in January 1933, the violence increased as the Nazis tried to remove all opposition. Two Nazi organisations were particularly important in the **police state**: the SS and the Gestapo.

From 1929 to 1945, the SS (*Schutzstaffel*) was led by Heinrich Himmler. It was a ruthless organisation responsible for crushing opposition to the Nazis. The SS ran the concentration camps and attacked Jews and other victim groups.

From 1934, the Gestapo was led by Reinhard Heydrich. The Gestapo encouraged people to spy on one another and report anyone who said or did things against the Nazis. Many Germans were terrified of the Gestapo because people could be arrested and sent to concentration camps based on rumours and without trial or explanation. New evidence shows that in some places in Germany as many as 80 per cent of the investigations carried out by the Gestapo started because of information voluntarily given by German people.

Heinrich Himmler, one of Hitler's closest and most trusted leaders, was Head of Police, the SS and the concentration camp system. After Hitler, he was the most powerful man in Germany.

He was obsessed with Nazi racial ideas. He played a leading role in the 'Final Solution', the plan to murder all the Jews of Europe.

In 1931, **Reinhard Heydrich** became the leader of the Security Service of the SS (SD). Its purpose was to spy on and root out Nazi enemies in Germany and abroad. In 1934, he also became the leader of the Gestapo. In 1939, Heydrich became chief of the Reich Security Main Office which was responsible for the Nazi plan to murder all Jews during the Second World War. He was a ruthless and brutal leader. He worked closely with his superior officer, Heinrich Himmler.

Think about

Are you surprised that the German people willingly gave information about each other to the Gestapo? Why might people have done this?

Concentration camps

In 1933, approximately 200,000 political opponents, mainly communists, were arrested because the Nazis saw them as a threat to their power. The Nazis had to quickly find places to imprison all these victims, so warehouses, factories, bars, hotels, castles and sports grounds were used. In the months and years that followed, the Nazis arrested hundreds of thousands of people who, they claimed, were enemies of Germany. Increasingly, these people were imprisoned in specially built concentration camps.

Between 1933 and 1945, the Nazis established 25 concentration camps with 1,100 smaller camps attached to them. On 22 March 1933, the first concentration camp opened near a town named Dachau, close to Munich. Murder was rare and most people were allowed to leave the camps after a period of time. But in all concentration camps living conditions were harsh, and beatings, humiliation, torture and

forced labour were common. Nazi guards were widely known for their brutality.

Figure 2.5 Secret photograph of Dachau prisoners marching through town (1933/34).

Think about

Concentration camps in Germany were not hidden. What does Figure 2.5 tell us about what German people knew about camps? Why might someone have taken this image of camp prisoners in secret?

FACTS AND STATISTICS

Early concentration camps

- They became a place where key political opponents like communists, could be removed from German society.

- As the camps were not hidden, they spread a climate of fear and terror across the country and discouraged people from challenging Nazi ideas and actions.

- At this time the majority of concentration camp prisoners were not Jews. Yet it is estimated that in 1933, five per cent of the prisoner population were Jewish. This means that Jewish people were five times more likely to be imprisoned in Nazi Germany than non-Jews.

How far did the German people support the Nazis?

The Nazis clearly used violence and terror to try to control Germany. But most historians agree that it is too simple to say the German people were 'forced' to support the Nazis because they were afraid. In fact, during the 1930s many Germans willingly supported the Nazis because they saw them as successful. For example, Hitler had promised to reduce unemployment and he succeeded. Nevertheless, there was a small number of people and organisations who did oppose the Nazis, though this became an increasingly difficult and dangerous thing to do.

Melita Maschmann

A teenager when Hitler came to power, Melita Maschmann joined a Nazi youth organisation. She spied for the Gestapo and gave them information about the family of her Jewish friend, Marianne Schweitzer. As a result, Marianne's elder sister was arrested and sent to a concentration camp. In 1963, Melita Maschmann published her memoirs about her support for the Nazis.

Source 2.1

Imagine all the families living in Berlin having scarcely enough dry bread to eat ... I believed the [Nazis] when they promised to do away with unemployment ... I believed them when they said they would reunite Germany, which had split into more than forty political parties, and overcome the consequences of the Treaty of Versailles.

Melita Maschmann, a German teenager

The Edelweiss Pirates

The Edelweiss Pirates were groups of young Germans who were opposed to the Nazis. They refused to behave as the Nazis wanted them to. Groups would go camping, sing anti-Nazi songs, fight with Nazi youth groups and during the war became involved in resistance activity. To begin with, their members were given warnings or were arrested but later, by the 1940s, they were sent to concentration camps. Some were even executed.

Source 2.2

Hitler's power may lay us low,

And keep us locked in chains,

But we will smash the chains one day.

We'll be free again.

An Edelweiss Pirates song

Figure 2.6 A group of Edelweiss Pirates posing by a lake, 1939/1940.

Source 2.3

The opening of a new motorway in 1937. Projects like this were used to create jobs. By 1936, unemployment was no longer a problem and, for many Germans, the future looked bright.

Activity

Did everyone support the Nazis? Explain your answer. Use the sources and case studies on pages 28–29 to help you.

Source 2.4

Konstantin Becker (second from the right), a teacher, refused to join the Nazi Party and the Nazi Teachers' Association. He also did not allow his children to join the Hitler Youth. The Nazi Party tried to have him dismissed but he continued to work at his school until it was closed in 1944.

2.3 Who did the Nazis see as enemies and how did they treat them?

Many different groups of people were targeted by the Nazis, but not always in the same way or for the same reasons. A very disturbing element of the Nazi worldview was the idea that some people ('races') were 'superior' to others. They incorrectly believed that science could identify 'pure blooded' Germans who were part of a 'master' or 'Aryan race'. The Nazis often persecuted, terrorised and even murdered those who were not regarded as part of the 'Aryan race' and the 'People's Community' (*Volksgemeinschaft*).

Activity
Enemies and threats

On these pages you will read short biographies of some of the victims. These will help you understand how and why the Nazis attacked particular groups. Read the accounts carefully and complete a table like the one started below.

Who?	Why were they seen as a threat to the Nazis?	How were they persecuted?	Which biography?
Helga Gross	Helga was a child with a hearing impairment. The Nazis believed that those with physical disabilities weakened Germany.	Helga was sterilised to prevent her from having children.	B

Biography A: The Kusserow family

Franz and Hilda Kusserow and their eleven children were **Jehovah's Witnesses**. The Nazis targeted Jehovah's Witnesses because they would not swear loyalty to Hitler. Two of the family's older sons were executed for refusing to serve in the army. The third son died after his release from the camps because of the terrible treatment he received. The three youngest children were put in Nazi-controlled foster homes for over six years. Other family members remained in concentration camps until the end of the war. Around 6,000

Jehovah's Witnesses from Greater Germany were held in prisons or concentration camps and around 1,400 died there. In addition, approximately 250 were executed for refusing to fight in the war.

Biography B: Helga Gross

Helga was a child with a hearing impairment. When she was 16, she was forced to be sterilised. The Nazis did not want her to have children and pass on what they claimed was her 'defect'. In July 1933 the Nazis introduced a law allowing for the compulsory sterilisation of those with illnesses that they believed could be passed onto future generations. They believed that people with physical disabilities weakened Germany and that their lives were worthless. Between 1933 and 1945 around 350,000 people were sterilised under this law without their consent. About 100 of these died as a result of the procedure. Helga survived but could not have children of her own. She moved to the USA in 1954.

Biography C: Rudolf Brazda

Born in Germany to Czech parents, Rudolf was arrested in 1937 for being gay and sentenced to six months in prison. Later, in 1941 he was arrested again and in 1942 sent to a concentration camp and subjected to hard labour and brutal treatment until 1945. The Nazis saw German gay men as a problem because they were unlikely to have children and help create a strong 'Aryan race'. Some Nazis also wrongly believed that being gay was something that could spread within Germany and corrupt German values. Gay men faced terrible treatment. Many were **castrated**. About 100,000 were arrested. Of those, 10,000–15,000 were placed in concentration camps where the majority died.

Biography D: Ludwig Neumann

Ludwig was a German Jewish businessman who owned an industrial clothing company. He was ordered to sell his factory in 1938 and was sent to Dachau concentration camp. The Nazis believed that Jews were racially inferior and dangerous to the 'Aryan race'. He was released on the understanding that he would leave Germany immediately. Ludwig Neumann **emigrated** to Britain.

Biography E: Bayume Muhammed Husen

© Marianne Bechhaus-Gerst

Bayume Muhammed Husen was born in German East Africa (now Tanzania). From 1929 he lived in Berlin and did several jobs to make a living. In 1941 he was denounced for having a relationship with a white German woman. The Nazis believed that people of the 'master race' should not mix with people of 'inferior' blood. He was arrested for 'racial disgrace' and taken to a concentration camp without trial. He died in the camp in 1944.

Biography F: Karl Stojka

Karl was born to Roma parents in Austria. His ancestors had travelled in family wagons across Austria for more than two hundred years. When Germany took control of Austria in 1938, his family had to stop travelling because the Nazis did not like the **Roma and Sinti** (so called 'Gypsies') way of life; they believed that it was criminal. The Nazis also wanted to prevent 'Gypsies' from mixing with 'Aryans'. In 1943, his family and tens of thousands of other Roma and Sinti were sent to camps. Many were later gassed, but Karl managed to survive the war.

Biography G: Anna Lehnkering

Anna (on the left in the photo) was born in Germany in 1915. When she was four years old she started having night terrors and anxieties. Later, she found learning at school difficult. In 1934, a year after the Nazis took power, Anna was forcibly sterilised because the Nazis saw her problems as a mental disability and didn't want her to have children. In 1936, she was taken to a so-called healing and care home. Then, in 1940, she was transported to Grafeneck Euthanasia Centre and murdered in a gas chamber.

From September 1939, the Nazis, with orders from Hitler, had begun to murder disabled children and later adults in Germany. The Nazis believed that people with mental or physical disabilities were worthless and made Germany weak. These murders were codenamed 'Aktion T4' and became known as the **'euthanasia' programme**. T4 staff and their methods were later used in the Holocaust.

UCL Centre for Holocaust Education

Now you have studied this unit, check your knowledge here:
www.ucl.ac.uk/holocaust-education

Develop knowledge and understanding

To deepen your knowledge and challenge common misunderstandings, you will learn:

- That during the 1930s the Nazis wanted to exclude German Jews from society.
- How the Nazis used **propaganda**, violence and anti-Jewish laws to make life extremely difficult for Jews in Germany.
- That the mass murder of Jews did not occur before 1939.
- About the impact that **persecution** had on Jews in Germany.
- How the geographic expansion of **Nazi Germany** affected Jewish people.
- How Jewish people responded to **discrimination**.
- About key historical events, such as the ***Anschluss*** and *Kristallnacht*.
- The challenges faced by Jewish people trying to leave Germany in the 1930s.

Think historically

Change and continuity

Consider what happened to Jews living in Germany during the 1930s.

Draw a timeline which begins in 1933, with Hitler being appointed leader of Germany, and ends in 1939 with the outbreak of the Second World War. Leave space to extend your timeline.

Mark on your timeline key events in the persecution of Jews in Germany.

When you think your timeline is complete, use it to answer the following questions:

- How did life for Jewish people change between 1933 and 1939?
- What aspects stayed the same?

Discuss

- Why did Nazi Germany become increasingly antisemitic? Was this just because the Nazis were in government, or were 'ordinary' Germans also responsible?
- How should we respond when a minority group has its freedoms and rights taken away?

The BIG question:
How and why did the Holocaust happen?

Look back at the notes you have previously written. As you are studying Unit 3, what new information, ideas or understanding do you have about this big question?

3.1 How did life change for German Jews?

Michael Siegel

Dr Michael Siegel was a German Jew who worked as a lawyer in Munich. When one of his clients was unlawfully arrested, he went to the police headquarters to make a complaint. There Michael was attacked by Nazi

Dr Siegel is forced to march through Munich by Stormtroopers, 10 March 1933.

Stormtroopers, who knocked out several teeth and burst one of his eardrums. Then, they hung a board around his neck which said, 'I will never again complain to the police' and marched him through Munich.

Activities

1 What can we learn from Michael Siegel's experience about the changes taking place in Germany in March 1933?

2 What are the similarities between the images on this page (Dr Siegel and Figure 3.1)? What messages do you think the Nazis were sending to the German people by discriminating against Germany's Jews in this way?

Early persecution

In the weeks and months after the Nazis came to power, thousands of Jews left Germany, but most decided to stay. Some didn't believe the Nazis would be in power for long. Others simply did not want to give up their homes and leave a country they loved.

At first, the Nazis appeared to be most concerned with crushing their **political opponents**. However, it was also very clear that they intended to put their antisemitic beliefs into action. Violence against Jewish people became more frequent, and discrimination against Jews soon became accepted.

Figure 3.1 On 1 April 1933, the Nazis tried to persuade people not to use shops owned by Jews. In this image, a crowd of Germans gather in front of a Jewish-owned department store in Berlin, 1 April 1933. Signs on the shop tell Germans not to buy from Jews.

Anti-Jewish laws

Antisemitism was a key part of Nazi ideology. While the Nazis saw various groups as enemies and threats (see page 30), they wrongly believed Jewish people were particularly dangerous. This was because, in their racist and troubling worldview, the Nazis saw Jews as an inferior but very powerful group who threatened the 'Aryan race'.

They also made other false claims about the number of Jewish people in Germany and their influence. From the racist perspective of the Nazis, this presented a 'problem': how should Jewish people be treated?

For much of the 1930s, the Nazis concentrated on excluding Jewish people from areas of German society. They did so by passing hundreds of anti-Jewish laws. In September 1935, this persecution took a new turn with the Nuremberg Laws. Now the Nazis said Jewish people were defined by their blood and could not therefore be German citizens.

Activity

Select the five laws from Figure 3.2 that you think were the most significant. Write a few sentences explaining your choices.

To help you with your explanation consider what was taken away by these laws, what Jewish people would no longer be able to do and how this might have impacted upon their lives.

1933
April 7 Jewish people working in government jobs are dismissed.
April 7 Jews are forbidden from entering the legal profession.
April 25 The number of Jewish children allowed in schools is limited.
April 25 Jews are not allowed to be members of sports clubs.
July 14 Jews in Germany who were born in other countries are no longer German citizens.
October 4 Jews are banned from being editors of newspapers.

1935
May 21 Jewish officers are **expelled** from the army.
September 15 Nuremberg Laws: German Jews are no longer German citizens. Jewish people are also not allowed to marry or have sex with non-Jews.
November 15 A Jew is defined as anyone with three grandparents who were born into a religious Jewish community.

1936
April 3 Jews are no longer allowed to be vets.
October 15 Jewish teachers are banned from schools.

1937
April 9 The Mayor of Berlin orders schools not to admit Jewish children until further notice.

1938
January 5 Jews are unable to change their names.
April 22 Jewish-owned businesses are forbidden from changing their names.
April 26 Any Jewish person with property of value has to report it.
July 11 Jews are banned from health spas.
August 17 Jews with 'non-Jewish' first names have to adopt an additional name: 'Israel' for men and 'Sara' for women.
October 3 Law passed which begins taking property owned by Jews and giving it to non-Jews.
October 5 Jews have to hand in their old passports, which only become valid after being stamped with the letter 'J'.
November 12 Jews are not allowed to own businesses, or to sell goods or services.
November 15 All Jewish children are expelled from schools.
November 29 Jews are forbidden to keep carrier pigeons.
December 3 Jews have their driving licences removed.
December 4 Jews are not allowed in cinemas or theatres.

1939
February 21 Jews are required to hand over to the government gold, silver, diamonds and other valuables, without **compensation**.
April 30 Local authorities are given power to evict Jews from rented houses or flats.
August 1 Jews are forbidden from buying lottery tickets.

Figure 3.2 A selection of anti-Jewish laws passed, 1933–39.

Living under the Nazis

All of the anti-Jewish laws passed by the government impacted people in real ways. Some of the laws affected Jewish people economically – that is, their ability to earn money. Other laws stopped Jewish people from living as other people did, restricting their freedoms. All of the laws helped to create an atmosphere of **prejudice** which spread across German society. Increasingly, Jewish people were treated – and made to feel – like they were 'different' from their non-Jewish neighbours.

Anti-Jewish propaganda – such as posters, newspapers, radio broadcasts and public speeches – helped spread messages of hate. Some non-Jewish Germans followed the lead and became hostile towards Jews. Others ignored it, or chose to accept it despite not agreeing with it. A few tried to work against growing antisemitism by offering support or help to the Jewish people they knew.

'Jews are not welcome here'

By the mid-1930s, new road signs began to appear in many towns and villages across Germany. Though the wording was different, the message was always the same: Jews are not welcome. Importantly, there was no law requiring these signs to be put up. Instead, local people in these places had chosen to do so.

Figure 3.3 'Jews here in Hildesheim unwanted' – sign outside Hildesheim, Lower Saxony.

Source 3.1

My sister and I used to slink by those huge banners that were all over the city. And we used to just try not to see them, thinking if we didn't see them, they weren't there. But they were there. That just, little by little, that really took over.

From the testimony of Gerda Haas

Antisemitic prejudice was not limited to road signs. It could be found in various other areas of German society too – from school textbooks to public parks; from board games to swimming pools.

Source 3.2

I was the only Jew in the school. They taught us 'race theory' every morning. Although I asked to be excused from these lessons, they wouldn't let me. Instead I got ten lashes.

From the testimony of Uri Ben Ari

Source 3.3

A board game called *Juden Raus!* ('Jews Out!'), released in 1938. Based in a city, players race to round up the Jews and remove them beyond the city walls.

Source 3.4

An unnamed woman sits on a public bench marked 'Only for Jews', Austria, March 1938.

Source 3.5

„Die Taufe hat aus ihm keinen Nichtjuden gemacht..."

A page from an antisemitic book called 'Trust no fox in the green meadow, and no Jew on his oath'. Written by a young schoolteacher and published in 1936, 100,000 copies of the book went to German schools. In it, Jews were falsely presented as being untrustworthy. Here, in an antisemitic caricature, a Jew has been baptised by a Christian vicar, but at the bottom of the page are the words 'Baptism didn't make him into a non-Jew ...' This was an important Nazi belief: that it didn't matter what Jewish people believed – according to their 'blood', they would always be Jewish.

Activities

Study the sources in the section 'Jews are not welcome here'.

1 Describe the different forms of antisemitic discrimination that you can identify.

2 Explain how each might have affected German citizens, both Jews and non-Jews.

Emigration

As the 1930s went on, it became clear that the Nazis would be in power for a while. Even so, although some Jewish people decided to **emigrate** to other countries, the majority stayed. Why didn't more Jews just leave?

Thousands of people did manage to emigrate. Typically, these people were young and had financial resources. Having money was an important factor: if a Jewish person emigrated, they had to pay a special exit tax on leaving the country and surrender their possessions, for which they received a very small fee. But money did not guarantee escape.

Few countries were willing to accept Jewish immigrants. Some worried that accepting immigrants might increase competition for jobs and make people angry. Many unfairly believed that if they let Jewish people in, then antisemitism in their country would increase.

Activity

Deciding to emigrate was not easy. And, of course, in the 1930s no one could possibly know or predict that persecution would turn into mass murder. Look at the illustration below. What do you think this family should do? Discuss the dilemmas facing this family with another student. Decide what you think they should do. Write a paragraph explaining your decision.

- We only speak German. It would be difficult to find a job in another country.
- I have been beaten up several times for no reason. This is happening more and more often.
- Recently we've been told we have to change our names. Why should we?
- I don't consider myself Jewish. But the government does. What's the point in staying?
- Our children are regularly picked on by their teachers and classmates.
- We are getting ill with worry about the future.
- We don't have a lot of savings.
- I still hope things in Germany will get better.
- What country will let us in?
- I am a German and I love Germany. I refuse to leave my country.
- If we left, we would have to depend on the help of relatives and friends to live. I don't like that.
- Some of our relatives feel too old to leave. What will happen to them if we go?
- I used to work for the government, but I lost my job for being 'Jewish'.

3.2 How were Jews affected by the creation of 'Greater Germany'?

The Nazis came to power promising to build a bigger and stronger Germany. Like many Germans, the Nazis believed Germany had been treated unfairly at the end of the First World War. They wanted to reclaim land they felt was Germany's and bring all German-speaking people together to live in a 'Greater Germany'. For the Nazis, this Greater Germany would be a national, People's Community (*Volksgemeinschaft*) – a society organised around ideas of 'race' (see page 21). Importantly, the Nazis did not believe Jewish people – among others – could or should be part of this new Germany.

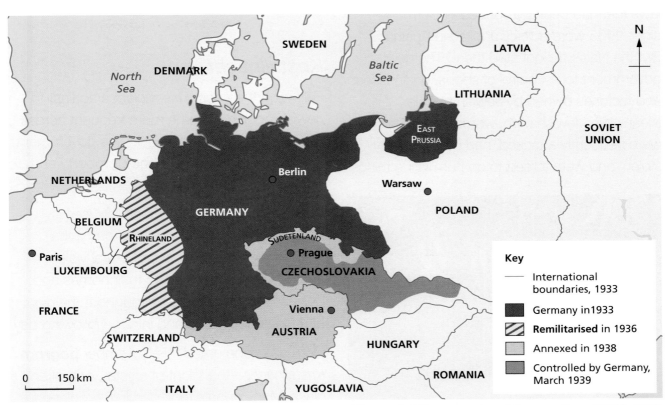

Figure 3.4 The expansion of Germany from 1933 to 1939.

Events in 1938–39

By the late 1930s, the Nazi government felt strong enough to act aggressively towards other countries. From March 1938, first Austria and then areas of Czechoslovakia became part of Germany. Each time Germany's borders expanded, more Jewish people fell under Nazi control.

The *Anschluss*

On 12 March 1938, the German army entered Austria. Most Austrians welcomed them. The people of Austria were asked if they wanted to become part of Germany. The vast majority did, so Austria officially became part of Germany. This was called the *Anschluss*.

At this time 180,000 Jews were living in Austria. Immediately Jewish people were targeted by both Nazis and Austrians. All of the anti-Jewish laws that had been introduced in Germany since 1933 were quickly applied in Austria. But the Nazis did not stop there. The new government took control of shops, businesses and factories owned by Jewish people. Meanwhile, Jewish men, women and children were frequently attacked, had their property stolen, and were forced to do humiliating things such as scrub the streets or eat grass from a park. By August, the Nazis took steps to try and make it quicker for Jewish people who wanted to emigrate to leave the country.

Figure 3.5 Supervised by members of the Hitler Youth, Jews are forced to scrub the streets in Vienna after the *Anschluss*.

> ## Activity
>
> Study Figures 3.5, 3.6 and 3.7. What do these photographs tell us about Jewish persecution in 1938?

Kristallnacht

Following the *Anschluss*, violence against Jewish people became more frequent across Greater Germany. Meanwhile, the government tried new ways to take money, property and business from Jews.

After a speech by Josef Goebbels (see page 23), members of the Nazi party, the SA and the SS led a wave of brutal violence against Jewish people and their homes and businesses which lasted throughout the night of 9 November 1938 and into the following day.

Germans soon called this November **pogrom** *Kristallnacht* – the 'night of crystal', or broken glass. Many people took part in the violence, but the government played a critical role.

The police were ordered not to interfere as thousands of shops, synagogues and homes across Greater Germany were destroyed or damaged. The Nazi government forced Jewish communities to pay for all the damage that had occurred.

Meanwhile, nearly 100 Jewish people were killed. Around 30,000 Jewish men were arrested and put in **concentration camps**. There they faced assault and torture, and were only released if they promised to leave Germany.

Think about

Why might historians describe *Kristallnacht* as a turning point in the Nazi persecution of Germany's Jews? How was *Kristallnacht* different from the ways in which Germany's Jews were discriminated against before 1938?

Figure 3.6 Jewish-owned businesses damaged during *Kristallnacht*.

Figure 3.7 Residents in Graz, Austria, watch as a Jewish synagogue burns.

Source 3.6

We came [back] to our home and there wasn't a chair for my grandmother to sit on … My aunt and I swept up the glass, tried to put some order. My grandparents did go next door. The Christian family opened their door and took them in and gave them breakfast.

From the testimony of Marga Randall

Source 3.7

When I looked out of the window eight to ten men [SA] were standing, heavily armed with axes, hatchets, daggers and revolvers … The mob arrived after the SA, then the school children; each party destroyed and stole yet more.

A Jewish businessman remembers *Kristallnacht*

Any hope Jewish people may have had that things might get better were crushed by the events of 1938. Hundreds of thousands desperately looked for ways to get out of Greater Germany. However, this was still very difficult to do.

Activity

How do Sources 3.6 and 3.7 describe the responses of ordinary German people to the events of *Kristallnacht*?

Figure 3.8 Roll call at the Buchenwald concentration camp for newly arrived prisoners, mostly Jews, arrested during *Kristallnacht*; Germany, 1938.

The Evian conference

In July 1938, officials from 32 countries – including Britain and the United States – met in Evian, France. They discussed ways to help the thousands of Jewish people trying to leave Germany. They all criticised the actions of the Nazis and expressed their sympathy for the Jews. However, apart from the Dominican Republic, no one was willing to remove restrictions on how many Jewish people they would allow into their country.

After *Kristallnacht*, some attempts were made to rescue Jews. However, despite being shocked by the violence of 1938, the world did little more to help the Jews of Germany.

One example of rescue was the *Kindertransport* (see page 82). The last *Kindertransport* left Berlin on 1 September 1939 – the day Germany invaded Poland. Two days later, Britain and France declared war. Most countries closed their borders completely during the war – those Jews still left in Greater Germany now had no chance to escape.

Think about

War and other human atrocities often create **refugees** – people who are forced to leave their homes for fear of their lives. What responsibility does the international community have to refugees?

Now you have studied this unit, check your knowledge here:
www.ucl.ac.uk/holocaust-education

UNIT 4 — Europe's Jews in the Second World War

Develop knowledge and understanding

To deepen your knowledge and challenge common misunderstandings, you will learn:

- That Jewish people had different experiences in different parts of occupied Europe.
- What **ghettos** were, why they were created, and what conditions were like in them.
- About how and why Germany invaded the Soviet Union and the brutal nature of war in the East.
- About how most Jewish people were killed in Eastern Europe from the start of 1942 to the middle of 1943.
- About who the ***Einsatzgruppen*** were and how they were involved in the murder of around 2.2 million Jewish people.
- Why the Nazis created **death camps**, where these were located, and how European Jews were murdered in them.
- That people all across Europe knew that Jews were being murdered.
- About when and how the Holocaust ended.

Think historically

Significance

Extend the timeline you drew in the previous unit, up to the end of the Second World War in 1945. Mark on your timeline important moments in the **persecution** and murder of Europe's Jews between 1939 and 1945. Explain your reasons for choosing the events you select.

When your timeline is complete, use it to answer the following questions:

- What changed in the way Jewish people were treated? Which events caused these changes?
- How important was the invasion of the Soviet Union?

Discuss

- How do you explain the different experiences of Jewish people during the Holocaust?
- Was the Holocaust a single event or was it a process?

The BIG question: How and why did the Holocaust happen?

Look back at the notes you have previously written. As you are studying Unit 4, what new information, ideas or understanding do you have about this big question?

4.1 What happened to the Jews of Europe at the beginning of the war (1939–41)?

On 1 September 1939, a week after signing a **neutrality agreement** with the Soviet Union, **Nazi Germany** invaded Poland. Two days later, Britain and France declared war on Germany. However, within a matter of weeks Poland had been defeated – in the west by the formidable German force, and in the east by the Soviet Union, which invaded on 17 October. In the nine months after the invasion of Poland in September 1939, the German army rapidly conquered much of Western and Northern Europe.

Everywhere the Nazis and their **allies** controlled, they discriminated against Jews. For example, Jews in many countries had to wear a star on their clothes, or an armband, that identified them as Jews. But the treatment of the Jews was not the same in all the countries under Nazi control or influence. The case studies on page 45 give examples of how Jews were treated in some of these countries.

Activity

Read the country case studies on page 45 and identify similarities and differences in the way Jews were treated in different European countries.

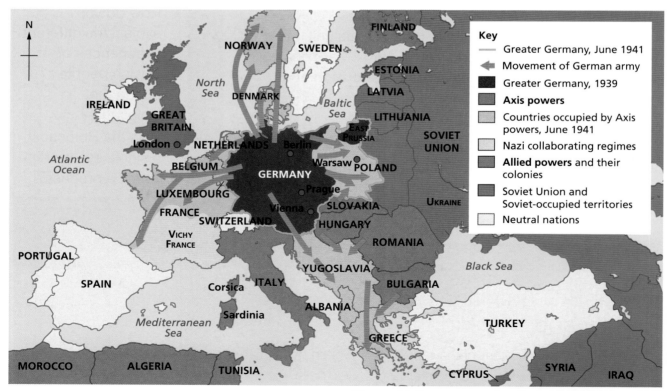

Figure 4.1 German expansion, September 1939–June 1941

Netherlands
Defeated: May 1940
Jewish population: approx. 160,000

After its surrender, the Netherlands was taken over by the SS. Jews were fired from their jobs in the civil service and businesses had to register their assets. Jewish students were **expelled** from schools and universities. In January 1941, all Jews had to register themselves as Jews. In February 1941, several hundred young Jews were arrested and sent to **concentration camps** in Germany.

France
Defeated: June 1940
Jewish population: approx. 350,000

The German army occupied northern and western France. In southern and eastern France, a (French) government was set up that collaborated with the Nazis (called the 'Vichy government'). In March 1941, Jewish property was taken away, leaving thousands homeless. In the autumn, both zones of France passed antisemitic laws, which were also applied in France's colonies in North Africa – Morocco and Algeria. Jews were no longer allowed to work as doctors, lawyers or teachers, or in industry and trade, the civil service or the military.

Denmark
Defeated: April 1940
Jewish population: approx. 7,500

The Nazis allowed the Danish government to continue to rule the country, as they saw Danish people as 'fellow Aryans'. The Danes protected their Jewish citizens. Throughout this period Jewish people in Denmark typically continued to live as they did before German occupation.

Romania
Joined the Axis powers: November 1940
Jewish population: approx. 600,000

In September 1940, a group of military officers and a fascist movement, the Iron Guard, seized power in Romania and joined the war. The government introduced antisemitic measures and took away Jewish property. Some Iron Guard members attacked Jews in the streets, robbing and sometimes killing them. In January 1941, dozens of Jewish civilians were murdered in Bucharest.

Germany
Jewish population: approx. 243,000

When the war started, the majority of German Jews had their jobs taken away. Jews were given a strict **curfew** and were not allowed to enter certain parts of many cities. They were also given reduced food **rations** and were only allowed to buy supplies from specific shops at specific times.

Hungary
Joined the Axis powers: November 1940
Jewish population: approx. 825,000

Between 1938 and 1941 the government passed laws against the Jews. Jews and non-Jews couldn't marry, and Jews were excluded from various jobs. In 1939, a forced-labour service was created for male Jews. Once Hungary joined the Axis powers, the labourers were sent to help the war effort. At least 27,000 subsequently died.

Due to the movement of people and borders during this period, it is difficult to know precise population figures. The figures here are estimates based on information from the United States Holocaust Memorial Museum.

4.2 What were ghettos and why were they created?

In September 1939, the German army attacked Poland and the Second World War started. Soon after the German army invaded Poland from the west, the Soviet army invaded the country from the east. This was a devastating attack and many hundreds of thousands of Polish people suffered and died. Very soon, Germany and the Soviet Union conquered all of Poland and divided it up between them.

Nazi-occupied Poland was named the 'General Government'. Within the General Government,

there were approximately 2 million Jews. In their racist view of the world, the Nazis regarded the large number of Polish Jews as a big problem. During a time of war, the Germans saw Jews as an even bigger threat to their security and so they wanted to control them. The Nazis also had the false belief that Jews spread diseases and should therefore be separated from others.

To try to deal with what the Nazis saw as a Jewish 'problem' in occupied Poland, Heydrich ordered that Jews should be moved to certain

Figure 4.2 Jews line up to move into the Warsaw ghetto. They were permitted to take only what they could carry (November 1940).

areas of towns and cities which would become ghettos. Entire communities were uprooted and **shtetls** devastated. Ghettos were sealed off from the rest of the world and the Jewish people inside could not leave or contact people outside.

Later, as the Nazis invaded and occupied other countries in the east of Europe, thousands more ghettos were created. Ghettos were considered to be a temporary solution to what the Nazis saw as the Jewish 'problem'. At that point, the Nazis wanted to remove the Jews from Europe but were not sure how.

Moving them to the island of Madagascar (off the south-east coast of Africa) was one of the options they were considering. The Madagascar plan was not new; it was first proposed in 1933.

Activities

1 Why did the Nazis create ghettos when they invaded Poland?

2 Why were ghettos a 'temporary solution'? What was the Nazis' plan for the Jews at this point in the war?

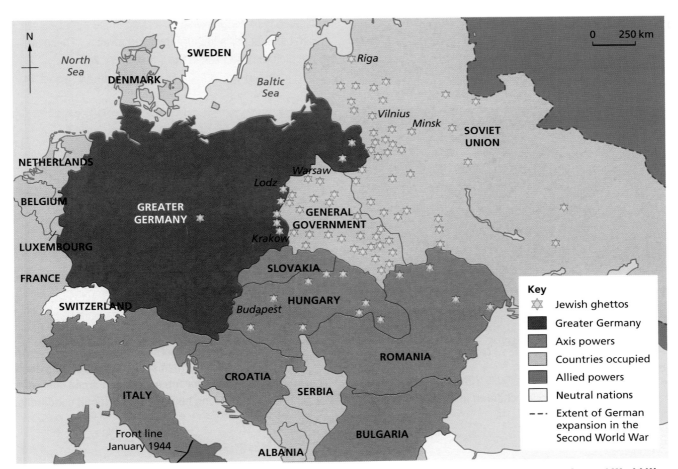

Figure 4.3 Examples of ghettos in occupied Europe during the Second World War.

The Warsaw ghetto

The largest ghetto in Nazi-occupied Europe was in Warsaw, Poland. It was in a very small part of the city – only a few streets – but around 460,000 Jews were violently moved from their homes and forced to live there.

Activity

The Warsaw ghetto was created in October 1940. In January 1941, 898 Jewish people died there. By August 1941, the number of deaths had increased to 5,560. Look at the images and sources on this page. Why do you think the death rate in the Warsaw ghetto increased so dramatically?

Source 4.1

The overcrowding in the ghetto was so catastrophic that on average seven to nine people shared each room, which meant that people were living with strangers.

Sheryl Silver Ochayon,
Holocaust educator

Source 4.2

From all around I hear voices calling out for bread. A tiny child, shivering all over, holds out his skinny hand and begs. His mother has died of hunger and the Germans have snatched his father for labour. And here is a poor woman whose clothes are torn and ragged, bloated with hunger, lying as if dead in the street. I can't look at her and I turn my head away … These are the pictures that I see in the street every day.

From the diary of Pepa Bergman, aged 14

Figure 4.4 Starving children in the Warsaw ghetto.

Figure 4.5 German soldiers transporting Jews from the ghetto for forced labour. Forced labourers worked long hours in very difficult conditions.

Jewish councils

In the ghettos, the Germans ordered the creation of Jewish councils (*Juderäte*). The councils were committees of important Jewish men. They had to 'run' the ghetto and carry out Nazi orders. They were also responsible for organising life in the ghetto. For example, they distributed food rations, medicines and other supplies, and they organised housing. Jewish councils were helped by the Jewish police force, whose job was to keep order in ghettos. The Jewish councils and police faced impossible dilemmas.

The Nazis used Jewish councils as a way of better controlling the population in the ghettos. In this way, they did not have to use many resources to police the Jews, as the councils did this work for them. What's more, the existence of Jewish councils gave the ghetto population a false sense of control over their own fate.

Activity

Research Chaim Rumkowski, the Jewish council leader of the Łódz ghetto. What are the similarities and differences between Czerniakow and Rumkowski? Leaders of Jewish councils have been figures of controversy. Why might this be?

Adam Czerniakow

Adam Czerniakow was the chairman of the Warsaw ghetto Jewish Council. His work included providing food, work, sanitation, housing and health services to the inhabitants of the ghetto. He co-operated with the Nazis and tried to keep them out of ghetto affairs as much as possible. He believed that this way more lives would be saved. Later on in the war, when the Nazis started to operate the death camps (see page 57), Czerniakow was ordered to round up Jews for **'resettlement'** to the East. Czerniakow – who knew that this meant death – refused to do it and took his own life. It is said that he left a note to his wife explaining his actions: 'They are demanding that I kill the children of my people with my own hands. There is nothing for me to do but to die.'

The Warsaw ghetto Jewish Council in a meeting. Adam Czerniakow is sitting third from the left.

4.3 What was the 'Holocaust by bullets'?

When the Second World War began, Germany and the Soviet Union were unlikely allies. Although they saw the world in opposite ways, they invaded Poland together – splitting the country in two. For the Nazis though, the alliance was only temporary: they still wanted to seize control of large parts of the Soviet Union for 'living space'. And they still believed the people of the Soviet Union were 'sub-human'.

Figure 4.6 German troops occupy a burning Russian village, summer 1941.

On Sunday 22 June 1941, Germany broke the neutrality agreement and invaded the Soviet Union. The invasion was called Operation Barbarossa. On the 12 July 1941, the Soviet Union and Britain announced an alliance against Germany and the **Axis powers**.

A racial war

The Nazis thought that most of the people who lived in the Soviet Union, the Slavs, were an inferior, 'sub-human race' of people. This led the Nazis to believe the normal rules of war did not apply. The war against the Soviet Union would serve two purposes.

1 It would allow the Nazis to gain land and resources, such as food and oil.

2 It would destroy communism, which the Nazis wrongly believed was led by Jews.

Operation Barbarossa was particularly brutal, with millions of civilians killed. Thousands of Roma and Sinti were also murdered in mass shootings.

Orders to murder

On 6 June 1941, the Chief of the Security Police, Reinhard Heydrich, issued a special order to the German army. Anyone who was believed to be a **communist** official, or who worked for the Soviet government, was either to be shot or handed over to special units called *Einsatzgruppen*.

A few weeks later, Heydrich sent instructions for the *Einsatzgruppen* to execute any communist politicians and all Jews employed by the Communist Party or government.

The *Einsatzgruppen* took Heydrich's instructions as an order to murder all Jewish men. Very quickly, however, women and children were targeted too and by mid-August were also being murdered.

The 'Holocaust by bullets'

By the summer of 1942, a new method for murder was being used in German-occupied Poland: death camps (see Chapter 4.4). But in the Soviet Union the *Einsatzgruppen* continued to kill people close to their homes, face-to-face, for the next two years.

By 1944, it is estimated they had murdered around 2,200,000 people. This policy of mass shooting has been called the 'Holocaust by bullets'.

Activities

1 Why was the invasion of the Soviet Union particularly brutal?

2 Revisit Chapters 4.1 and 4.2. What were the similarities and differences in the experiences of Jews living in the East of Europe and Jews living in the West of Europe? Where were Jews in most danger between 1939 and 1941?

FACTS AND STATISTICS

The *Einsatzgruppen*

- There were four *Einsatzgruppen* – A, B, C and D.

- Their main function in the Soviet Union was to murder Jewish men, women and children.

- In any one *Einsatzgruppe* there were between 600 and 1,000 men. These men were then split into smaller groups.

- They were made up of men from an armed SS force called the Waffen SS, and from the German security services.

- They were helped by thousands of others – possibly as many as a quarter of a million people. This included the German army, German police units, and local people living in Eastern Europe.

- *Einsatzgruppen* A, B and C were attached to an army group and worked across the Soviet Union. *Einsatzgruppe* D went to the south of Ukraine.

- They submitted regular reports to Heydrich.

- They encouraged local people to act violently towards their Jewish neighbours.

- The *Einsatzgruppen* murdered in two 'sweeps'. The first was from June 1941 to the winter of 1941. Around 500,000 people were murdered in this time. The second began in spring 1942 and ran until the summer. During the second 'sweep', thousands of non-military German policemen were sent to support the *Einsatzgruppen*.

The process of murder tended to follow a standard pattern:

On arriving in a town or village, Jews were ordered to assemble in a particular place, at a given time, on a given date. They were told to bring possessions and clothes. If necessary, the local mayor was asked for a list of Jews living in the town or village.

Members of the *Einsatzgruppen* surrounded the town or village, preventing escape. As Jews gathered at the assembly point, houses were searched to ensure no one was hiding. Jews would be taken in groups to a site on the edge of the town or village – often a graveyard or a forest.

Jewish people were told to stand by or lie down in the trench or pit. They were then shot by a firing squad. When the trench or pit was full of bodies, it was filled in with earth. The victims' possessions were taken away or sold to local people.

At the site, Jews were forced to undress and hand over their possessions. Anyone refusing to do so would be killed immediately. The Jewish people would then be taken to a trench or a pit.

Figure 4.7 How the *Einsatzgruppen* operated.

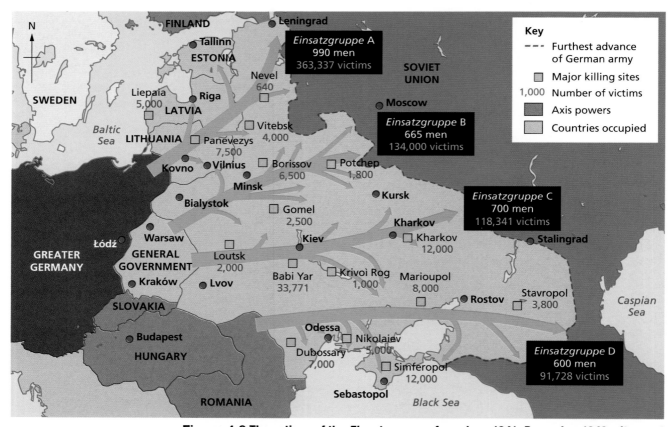

Figure 4.8 The actions of the *Einsatzgruppen* from June 1941–December 1942 – its most intensive period of activity. The total number killed by each *Einsatzgruppe* during this time is shown in orange. Murder continued until 1944, with hundreds of thousands more killed.

Babi Yar – A case study

Dina Pronicheva was born in 1911 into a poor Jewish family living in Kiev, in modern-day Ukraine. After marrying a non-Jewish Russian named Viktor, she had two children. Dina worked in Kiev's Puppet Theatre for children.

When war broke out between Nazi Germany and the Soviet Union, Viktor left to join the Soviet army. Dina stayed in Kiev with her two young children, her parents and her sister. On 19 September 1941, the Germans arrived in the city. Nine days later, Dina saw posters ordering all Jews to report the next day. They were to bring their documents, possessions and warm clothes. Anyone who failed to report would be shot. People thought they were being moved somewhere else.

On 29 September, Dina dropped her children off with her mother-in-law. She wanted to go with her parents and sister to the assembly point to see them off. Once there, however, she was caught up in the crowd of thousands of people who were walking towards a ravine on the outskirts of the city, known as Babi Yar.

> Ahead of me a woman with two children in her arms walked along, while the third clung to her apron strings. The sick women and elderly

Dina Pronicheva

people were taken by carts, on which bags and suitcases were piled up. Small children were crying.

> Dina Pronicheva

When she arrived at the site, Dina tried to use the Russian surname on her passport to claim she was not Jewish. Although she was believed at first, Dina was later marched to the edge of the mass grave. As the shooting began, Dina threw herself into the pit and pretended to be dead. Then, while the Germans checked for survivors, she crawled out of the grave and escaped. Dina was one of the very few who managed to survive.

> I saw a young woman, completely naked, nursing her naked baby when a policeman came running up to her, tore the baby from her breast, and threw it into the pit alive. The mother rushed there after her baby. The [policeman] shot her and she fell down dead …
>
> Dina Pronicheva

Across two days, members of *Einsatzgruppe* C murdered 33,771 Jewish men, women and children at Babi Yar. It was one of the largest single acts of murder during the Holocaust.

Think about

What do we learn about the 'Holocaust by bullets' from the events at Babi Yar?

Figure 4.9 The perpetrators at Babi Yar root through the possessions of the victims, 1 October 1941.

Johannes Hähle

Johannes was a photographer who joined the Nazi party in 1932 when he was 26. In 1941, after being drafted into the armed forces, he was attached to the army invading the Soviet Union. His job was to take **propaganda** photographs. But he also took other photographs, with a colour film, that he kept private. When he arrived in Kiev, he took 29 colour photographs from Babi Yar, including Figure 4.9. Johannes died in 1944. He never showed anyone the photographs from Babi Yar, and his wife inherited them. She sold black and white copies of them to a journalist in the 1950s.

Activity

Revisit the previous chapters in this unit. How was the 'Holocaust by bullets' different from what had happened before?

Think about

What are your views on the actions of Johannes and his wife?

4.4 What was the 'Final Solution'?

For the Nazis, victory in Eastern Europe would create an opportunity for them to 'solve' things that they wrongly believed were problems. In the Nazis' racist worldview, one of the main 'problems' was what to do with the Jewish people who were under their control. However, even among Nazis there were different views over what to do. All believed a 'final solution' to the Jewish 'problem' was needed.

Murder moves westwards

Herbert Lange

Herbert Lange was a policeman who joined the Nazi Party in 1932 and the SS in 1933. In 1939–40, Lange was in charge of a group that murdered people who were classified by the Nazis as 'disabled' in the Warthegau – an area of German-occupied Poland. The group came up with the idea of gassing these people in converted vans.

Arthur Greiser

Arthur Greiser was governor of the Warthegau. Greiser wanted to make the Warthegau free of Jews, most of whom were now living in ghettos. He tried and failed to do this by moving Jews into other parts of German-occupied Poland. Eventually, he decided to achieve his goal through murder.

In the summer of 1941, once Hitler and Himmler had given their permission, Greiser and his officials began drawing up plans. Mass shootings began in September, but a new method of killing was introduced. In 1939 and 1940, gas vans had been used to kill thousands who were classified by the Nazis as 'disabled' in Germany and German-occupied Poland. It was decided this would be the best way to make the Warthegau 'free' from Jews.

Activities

1 Why did Greiser decide to murder Jews in the Warthegau?

2 What can we learn about the decision-making process behind the Holocaust from the events in the Warthegau?

Chelmno

Figure 4.10 View of the village of Chelmno, taken sometime between 1939 and 1943. The mansion is visible on the left of the photograph (next to the church and its spire).

In the autumn of 1941, Herbert Lange was given the job of killing those Jews in the Warthegau who could not be used as slave labour. He chose Chelmno, a small village of around 250 people, as the site for a new camp (see Figure 4.10) based in a mansion in the middle of the village. On 8 December, a group of nearby Jews were rounded up and driven to the mansion. They were told they were being sent for work, but needed to shower. They undressed, left their valuables and were then guided into the back of a van. The doors closed and gassing began. After around ten minutes, the van drove to a forest where the bodies were buried or burnt.

Small groups of men were kept alive to do work, including taking victims to the gas vans, cleaning the vans and sorting through possessions. When not working, they would be kept locked in a room in the basement (see Figure 4.11). Periodically, these men would themselves be killed.

Figure 4.11 A group of Jewish men, likely to be members of a labour squad, at the mansion in Chelmno, sometime between 1941 and 1943.

By the time the Germans left Chelmno in January 1945, at least 172,000 Jewish people had been killed there. Many came from the Łódź ghetto.

Simon Srebrnik

Simon was deported to Chelmno from the Łódź ghetto when he was 13 years old. He was put in chains and selected to sort clothes and valuables, burn bodies and take the ashes of victims in a boat and dump them down river. Simon was well known by people living in Chelmno. In January 1945, he managed to escape.

Activities

1 Who developed the method of mass murder used at Chelmno?
2 How was the murder of Jews at Chelmno connected to the murder of another victim group?

Source 4.3

There were many handbags, a mountain of handbags. Once, I found a handbag with my mother's pictures and all her documents.

From the testimony of Simon Srebrnik

Think about

Do you think that the people of Chelmno knew what was happening at the death camp?

The death camps

Chelmno was the first death camp in history. Its sole purpose was to murder. Even those who were kept alive for slave labour would be killed eventually. This was the underlying idea of a death camp. No one was meant to survive.

Chelmno began because of the ambitions of Arthur Greiser. But by the time Chelmno opened, the idea of murdering Jews was widely accepted among the Nazi leadership. We do not know when exactly, and no written order exists, but by the winter of 1941, decisions had been made to co-ordinate the killing already taking place in the Warthegau and the Soviet Union and to include Jews living in Western Europe.

In 1942, other death camps opened in German-occupied Poland (see Figure 4.12). Located close to major train routes to make them accessible, these camps were often in quite remote areas. However, those who lived nearby knew what happened there and rumours soon spread across Europe.

Like Chelmno, murder was by gas, but not in vans: instead, people were killed in specially built chambers either by the fumes of engines or – as at Auschwitz-Birkenau – by poison gas.

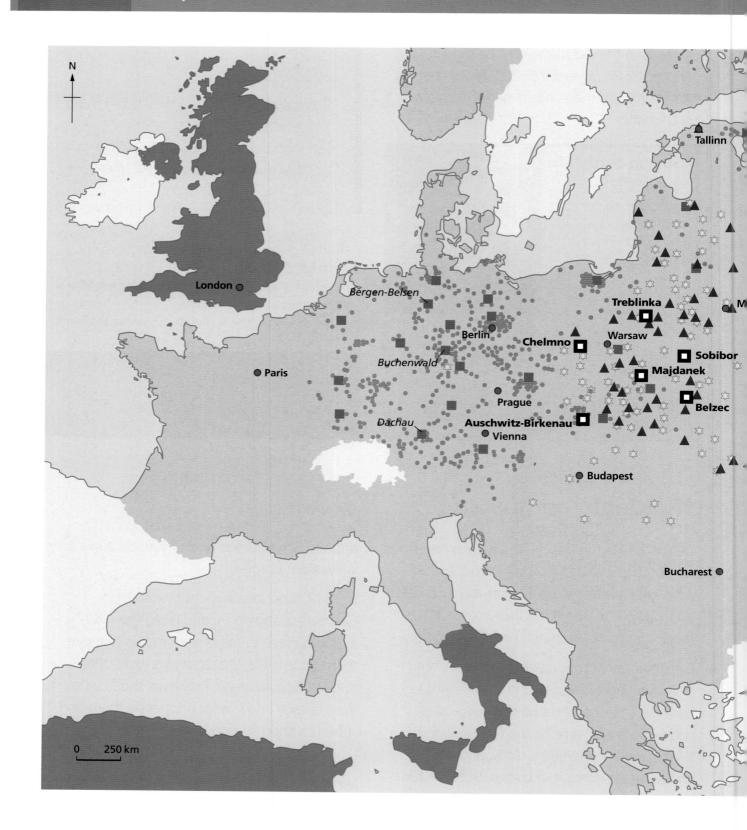

N

London

Bergen-Belsen

Berlin

Buchenwald

Paris

Dachau

Prague

Auschwitz-Birkenau

Vienna

Tallinn

Treblinka

Warsaw

Chelmno

Sobibor

Majdanek

Belzec

Budapest

Bucharest

M

0   250 km

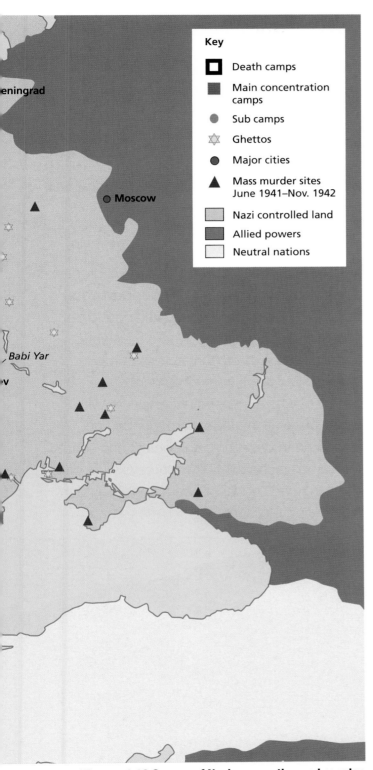

Figure 4.12 Spaces of Nazi persecution and murder.

The six main death camps in Nazi-occupied Poland

Chelmno
Operational: December 1941–March 1943/ April–July 1944

c. 172,000 victims

Belzec
Operational: March–December 1942

434,500 victims

Auschwitz-Birkenau
Operational: Spring 1942–January 1945

1,100,000 victims

Sobibor
Operational: May 1942–November 1943

170,000–250,000 victims

Treblinka
Operational: July 1942–September 1943

870,000 victims

Majdanek
Operational: October 1942–December 1943

78,000 victims

Think about
Study Figure 4.12. What does the map tell us about the geography of the Holocaust? What questions does it raise?

The Wannsee Conference

By the end of 1941, hundreds of thousands of Jewish people in Eastern Europe had been killed. Murder had started to move westwards (see page 55), while Nazi leaders were worried that the war against the Soviet Union was not going well. At some point in the last few months of 1941, it was decided that the 'Final Solution' to the 'Jewish problem' was mass murder. **Genocide** would now be pursued across Europe.

On 20 January 1942, fifteen leading Nazis and German officials met at a villa near Berlin. The Wannsee Conference was a meeting to discuss how different government departments would work together to deport Jewish people from across Europe and take them to the death camps.

The meeting was led by Heydrich, who emphasised that the SS would be in charge and demanded everyone's cooperation.

An intense wave of murder followed. Over the next 12 months, millions were killed. In Nazi-occupied Poland alone, for instance, 1.2 million Jews were murdered in a programme codenamed Operation Reinhard.

Activities

1 What was the purpose of the Wannsee Conference?

2 What was different about death camps, compared to the 'Holocaust by bullets'?

Think about

On 20 July 1944, Jewish people living on the Greek islands of Rhodes and Kos were put on a boat to the mainland. From there, they travelled for nearly two weeks by train to Auschwitz-Birkenau. How many countries did these people pass through? What does this tell us about the Nazi plan to destroy Jewish life across Europe?

Deportation

With the decision to murder as many European Jews as possible, a process of **deportation** began. People living in ghettos started to be sent to the death camps, where they were to be joined by Jews from across Europe. Transporting Jews from all corners of the continent was a massive undertaking. With local cooperation, Jews were rounded up, placed on trucks, trains and boats, and sent to the camps in the East. The journeys were often very long and conditions were appalling. Many died during the journey.

Figure 4.13 Jews boarding a train to the East at Westerbork, in the Netherlands.

Auschwitz-Birkenau

Activity

What do you know about 'Auschwitz'? Work with a partner and compile a list of all you know.

1940
The Nazis change the name of Oświęcim in Poland to 'Auschwitz'.

The SS convert some existing army barracks into a concentration camp for Polish political prisoners.

This becomes 'Auschwitz I' (the camp with the brick buildings you can see today).

New camps and sub-camps are built in and near the town, each with a different purpose. One, intended for Soviet prisoners of war, is called Auschwitz-Birkenau.

Building work begins in October 1941.

By early 1942, plans had changed; it was to become a death camp for Jews and others.

In spring 1942, a farmhouse is converted to a gas chamber.

By summer, another larger gas chamber opens in another former farmhouse.

In these buildings, thousands were killed by the Nazis and their **collaborators** but they could not cope with the number of people being sent to them.

In February 1943 thousands of Roma are deported to Auschwitz-Birkenau. They are placed in a so-called 'Gypsy Family Camp'. Around 22,000 people are imprisoned here before it is closed in August 1943. Thousands die from disease or are killed in the gas chambers.

By March 1943, four new buildings open, each containing a gas chamber and crematoria ovens for burning bodies.

By summer 1943, it was now possible for around 150,000 people to be killed each month at Auschwitz-Birkenau.

Figure 4.14 SS photograph of cement being poured during the construction of Crematorium III at Auschwitz-Birkenau, 1942–43.

The majority of Europe's Jews were murdered between March 1942 and February 1943. Death mainly came at the hands of the *Einsatzgruppen*, from starvation and disease in ghettos, or by gas in the death camps. By the summer of 1943, the deadliest place for Jews in Europe was Treblinka. There, around 700,000 people had been murdered since July 1942. In 1944, this changed when the death camp at Auschwitz-Birkenau became the destination of the largest remaining Jewish community in Europe: the Jews of Hungary.

Activity

Return to your list of things you know about 'Auschwitz'. Do you need to revise any of these ideas? What new information can you add?

Case study: Hungary, 1944

In March 1944, Germany invaded Hungary to stop it from making peace with the Allied powers. Under Nazi pressure, a new government took over and it was committed to deporting the Jews. Very quickly, Hungarian Jews were put into ghettos. In May, these began to be emptied and Jewish men, women and children were put on trains headed for Auschwitz-Birkenau.

In a matter of six weeks, 430,000 people had arrived at the death camp. The camp struggled to cope. The gas chambers and crematoria worked through the night. Bodies were burned in the open. A new railway spur was built so that trains could take Jews directly to the gas chambers.

By the time the Soviet army liberated Budapest in January 1945, around 565,000 Hungarian Jews had been murdered.

Figure 4.15 Bodies being burnt in the open at Auschwitz-Birkenau, August 1944. This photograph was taken in secret by a Jewish man forced to work in the gas chamber. The camera was smuggled into the camp by the Polish resistance movement. The photograph is one of the few we have of the killing process at Auschwitz-Birkenau. The victims are believed to be Hungarian Jews.

Activities

Look at the photograph taken at Auschwitz-Birkenau in 1944 (Figure 4.15) and Eva's diary entry.

1 What is the value of the photograph? Why is it significant? What questions does it raise?

2 Did Eva believe what she and her grandparents were told about being resettled? What does her diary reveal about how much people knew and understood in 1944?

Eva Heymann

On 13 February 1944, 13-year-old Eva started writing a diary. She was living in Nagyvárad, Hungary, with her grandparents following her parents' divorce. Her dream was to be a newspaper photographer.

Eva and her grandparents were forced into the city's ghetto in April 1944. On 29 May, they were told they were going to be 'resettled in the East'. Eva made her last diary entry the next day:

'… Dear diary, I don't want to die; I want to live even if it means that I'll be the only person allowed here to stay […] I can't write anymore, dear diary, the tears run from my eyes'.

A few days later, Eva and her grandparents were taken to Auschwitz-Birkenau, where they were murdered on 17 October 1944.

4.5 When and how did the Holocaust end?

The Holocaust only ended with the defeat of Nazi Germany. From the summer of 1944, the wartime **Allied powers**, the Soviet Union in the east and Britain and the USA in the west and the south, forced the German army to retreat after a series of defeats.

The death marches

As the German army retreated, those prisoners still alive in the remaining camps began to be moved away from the approaching Allied forces to other concentration camps, **work camps** and their **sub camps** inside Germany and Austria. The Nazis wanted to make sure there were no witnesses to their crimes. Also, they still wanted to use Jewish prisoners as slave labour.

Prisoners were either forced to walk, often for weeks at a time, or were herded into tightly packed freight trains, made for goods not people. There was no shelter and they were given little, if any, food and water. Those prisoners who could not keep up or who tried to escape were shot. Conditions on these forced marches were so terrible that the prisoners themselves gave them the name 'death marches'. In total, approximately 250,000 prisoners, both Jews and non-Jews, died as a result of the death marches.

Think about

What do Figure 4.16 and Source 4.5 on the next page tell us about what German civilians knew and how they treated prisoners? Why might some German civilians have taken such photographs in secret?

Figure 4.16 Death march from Dachau. German civilians secretly photographed several death marches as they passed through their towns.

Source 4.4

For nine days I had been walking completely barefoot in the snow … The transport commander selected all the bare-footed and put them in the carts with the sick. Calmly he told us that we would be shot within half an hour … We were not shot … We were put into open cattle cars for three days and three nights … On the way, 75 per cent of us were frozen.

From the testimony of Elisabeth Herz

Source 4.5

The area was German, and the local Hitler Youth groups threw stones at them [the prisoners] … as they passed through the townships. The German peasants refused to lodge them [the prisoners] in stables. They are afraid of the 'Jewish devils'; the girls had to sleep in the field, in the snow. In Christianstadt German women tried to give us bread. But the women guards wouldn't permit it … The brutal woman guard yelled: 'What are you doing, pitying Jews?'

From the testimony of Aliza (Frunka) Besser

Liberation

As they advanced towards Germany, the Allied forces found victims of the death marches. They also found death camps, concentration camps and work camps. Soldiers were horrified by what they found. Because of starvation, disease and brutal treatment, the few surviving prisoners were very close to death. Evidence of mass murder and torture was there for the world to see.

On 7 May 1945, the Germans surrendered to the British and Americans. Two days later, on 9 May 1945, Germany surrendered to the Soviets. The Second World War in Europe was over. For the few prisoners left alive in the camps, this meant freedom and the chance of survival. Yet for many, **liberation** came too late. Weak from starvation, disease, torture and forced labour, liberated prisoners continued to die.

Treblinka

The Nazis had destroyed the death camps at Treblinka, Sobibor and Belzec in 1943. This was because they had completed their task in murdering the majority of Poland's Jews. Soviet troops reached the site of Treblinka during the last week of July 1944. A farmhouse was now built on the site and the ground was ploughed. Despite the Nazis' attempts to hide the mass murder that took place there, the Soviets found small pieces of bone, human teeth and the belongings of those murdered.

A Soviet soldier (on the right) stands next to evidence of mass murder at the site of the Treblinka death camp.

Auschwitz-Birkenau

Attempts to hide evidence of mass murder increased as Germany began to lose the war and retreat. At the end of October 1944, the gas chambers at Auschwitz-Birkenau were closed, and in November Himmler ordered their destruction. The chaos of this time meant that in some places evidence wasn't destroyed and the ruins of gas chambers remained at some camps but not at others. On 27 January 1945, the Soviets liberated Auschwitz-Birkenau and the 7,000 prisoners who remained alive there.

The ruins of crematorium and gas chamber II at Auschwitz-Birkenau. The image shows the entrance to the changing room.

Bergen-Belsen

On 15 April 1945, the British liberated Bergen-Belsen concentration camp. Sixty thousand emaciated and sick prisoners were in desperate need of medical attention. More than 13,000 dead prisoners lay unburied around the camp, victims of starvation, disease and Nazi brutality. Roughly two-thirds of those found alive were Jewish. Many of these were survivors of forced death marches from death camps in the East, especially Auschwitz-Birkenau.

A woman inmate of Bergen-Belsen concentration camp kisses the hand of Army Film & Photographic Unit cameraman Lieutenant Martyn Wilson on liberation.

Dachau

On 27 April 1945, as American troops approached the area around Dachau concentration camp, 7,000 prisoners, mostly Jews, were forced to begin a death march away from the camp. Just two days later, on 29 April 1945, after a brief battle with the remaining SS guards, the camp was liberated by the Americans. They discovered 30,000 survivors, most severely emaciated. There were also 9,000 dead prisoners found at the camp.

Prisoners liberated by the Americans inside Dachau concentration camp.

UCL
Centre for
Holocaust
Education

Now you have studied this unit, check your knowledge here:
www.ucl.ac.uk/holocaust-education

Develop knowledge and understanding

To deepen your knowledge and challenge common misunderstandings, you will learn:

- How Jewish people responded to their **persecution**, fought back and resisted the Nazis and their **collaborators**.
- How hundreds of thousands of people from across Europe were involved with the persecution and murder of Europe's Jews.
- That responsibility for the Holocaust was much wider than just Hitler and a few leading Nazis.
- About how some countries and some people tried to help Jews, but many did not.
- That those who refused to obey orders to kill Jews were not shot, but given other duties.
- What the British government knew about the persecution and murder of Europe's Jews and how they responded.
- That Britain did not fight the war to save Europe's Jews but argued the best way to help them was to defeat **Nazi Germany** and win the war.

Think historically

Interpretation

Different interpretations exist about the extent to which ordinary German people – and people in other occupied countries – were responsible for the Holocaust.

This issue is debated by two history students:

> *Student 1:* Hitler and leading Nazis were responsible for the Holocaust. It was their idea and they ordered it to be carried out.

> *Student 2:* The Holocaust only happened because of the actions of hundreds of thousands of people from all across Europe. Some people killed, many participated and others just stood by as Jews were persecuted and murdered.

What evidence exists to support the two interpretations? Which one do you agree with most? Why?

Discuss

- During the Holocaust people had to make choices. What caused people to respond differently and make different choices? What does this tell you about human behaviour?
- How significant was **antisemitism** as an explanation of why so many people were willing to kill Jews?

Concluding the BIG question: How and why did the Holocaust happen?

Once you have studied all the information in Units 1 to 5, you should be in a position to provide a concluding answer to the BIG question – can you explain how the Holocaust happened and the main reasons why it occurred?

5.1 Did the Jews fight back?

Against impossible odds, many Jews did fight back and resist the Nazis and their collaborators. Resistance occurred across Europe. It took place in **ghettos**, **concentration camps** and **death camps** in every German-occupied country.

Acts of resistance in the ghettos

Conditions in the ghettos were appalling (see pages 46-49). The Nazis did not treat Jews as human beings. They tried to stop them from leading normal lives. For example, anyone caught doing ordinary things like holding religious services, going to school or listening to the radio could be shot. For this reason, simple acts like those shown in the word cloud and photographs on this page were important acts of resistance by Jews in ghettos.

Taking photographs   Caring for   Going to
Painting and   the elderly   concerts
drawing   Talking with   Teaching children
friends   Reading newspapers
Saying prayers   Getting married
Keeping   RESISTANCE   Studying
diaries
Sharing food   Looking after   Staging plays
Listening to   the sick   Writing stories
the radio   Hiding from   and poems
the enemy   Singing songs
Going to 'school'   Attending religious services

Figure 5.2 Celebrating the festival of Hanukkah in the Łódź ghetto, 1943.

Figure 5.1 Children secretly studying in a school in the Kovno ghetto, 1941–42.

Figure 5.3 An SS man searching a Jewish child trying to smuggle food into the Warsaw ghetto, 1939. Smuggling food was a very important form of resistance as it helped people survive.

The Ringelblum archive

We know about resistance in the ghettos from the **testimony** of survivors and because Jewish groups documented life there. For example, historian Dr Emanuel Ringelblum and his trusted friends recorded life in the Warsaw ghetto. As you can see from Figure 5.4, he hid the information as a record for future historians. This incredible collection, discovered after the war ended, is full of documents, literature, photographs, drawings, theatre posters, songs, plays, programmes and other evidence. The contents show the courage and determination of Jews in the ghettos to lead 'normal' lives in terrible circumstances.

> **Think about**
>
> Some people think that 'resistance' only involves fighting with force. Do you agree? Explain your answer.

Activities

1 What were Jewish people aiming to achieve by the activities shown in the photographs in this chapter?

2 Talking about life in the ghetto, Holocaust survivor Esther Brunstein once said, 'To have survived one day under those conditions and retain one's values was a great act of resistance.' What did she mean by this statement?

3 Why did Dr Emanuel Ringelblum create the secret archive? How useful is it to historians?

Figure 5.4 The secret archive created by Emanuel Ringelblum is discovered after the war.

Figure 5.5 A portrait of a girl, painted by artist Gela Seksztajn in the Warsaw ghetto and found in the Ringelblum archive.

Right and below: from E. Ringelblum Jewish Historical Institute, Warsaw, Poland

Figure 5.6 Poster (1941) found in the Ringelblum archive. It advertises two concerts by the Jewish Symphonic Orchestra to be held in the ghetto.

Armed resistance in camps and ghettos

Fighting back against the Nazis was incredibly difficult. The guards at camps and ghettos were well-trained and heavily armed. Jews often did not have the strength, opportunity, weapons and training to fight back. Fighting back would lead to certain death. Also, the Nazis often killed not only Jews who fought back, but also their family, friends and neighbours.

Despite the reasons listed above, as the map shows, it is remarkable how often Jews in ghettos and camps *did* fight back. Between 1941 and 1943, organised resistance movements sprang up in 100 Jewish ghettos in Nazi-occupied Eastern Europe. They organised attacks against the Nazis and their **allies**, and helped some Jews escape from the ghettos.

Most Jews were gassed as soon as they arrived at death camps but some were kept as prisoners. Because Jewish prisoners were weak and unarmed, resistance in the death camps was very rare. Incredibly, however, some resistance did take place (see Figure 5.7). Here are three examples:

- In **Treblinka** (August 1943), Jewish prisoners seized weapons, set camp buildings on fire and rushed the main gate. Many were killed by machine-gun fire. Although more than three hundred did escape, most were tracked down and killed.

- In **Sobibor** (October 1943), a dozen guards were killed by Jewish prisoners and around three hundred escaped. Most were later recaptured and killed, but about fifty did escape and survived the war.

- In **Auschwitz-Birkenau** (October 1944), 250 prisoners blew up buildings, attacked the camp guards and escaped to the nearby forest. They were all hunted down and recaptured.

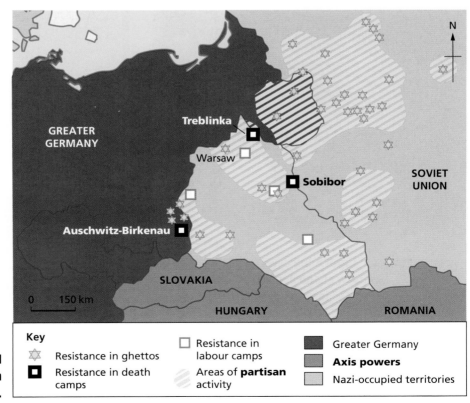

Figure 5.7 Jewish armed resistance in Eastern Europe, 1941–44.

Key
- ✡ Resistance in ghettos
- ◼ Resistance in death camps
- ☐ Resistance in labour camps
- ◿ Areas of **partisan** activity
- ▨ Greater Germany
- ▨ **Axis powers**
- ▨ Nazi-occupied territories

The Warsaw ghetto uprising, April–May 1943

One of the most significant acts of armed resistance took place in the Warsaw ghetto in April 1943. During the previous summer, more than 260,000 Jews were deported from the ghetto and murdered in Treblinka. Around 60,000 Jews remained in the ghetto.

On 19 April 1943, German troops and police entered the ghetto to deport those still living there. But they were immediately shot at by Jewish fighters using guns that had been smuggled into the ghetto. The troops were forced to retreat. Led by 23-year-old Mordechai Anielewicz, Jewish resistance lasted for almost a month.

In response, the ruthless German forces burned the ghetto – building by building – and forced Jews out of their hiding places. By 16 May 1943, the Germans had killed 7,000 Jews (including Anielewicz) and destroyed the ghetto. Those who were captured were sent to forced labour camps or murdered in Treblinka death camp.

Figure 5.8 Jews captured during the Warsaw ghetto uprising are led away from the burning ghetto by SS guards.

Activities

1 Create a list of risks and dangers that Jews faced when considering whether or not to fight back. Why was it so difficult for Jews to fight back?

2 The three accounts of resistance in the death camps are brief. Use the internet to find out more about the three events of armed resistance in the death camps in 1943 and 1944. Write a report of events at each one.

Think about

Jews who fought back in the Warsaw ghetto uprising knew they would almost certainly be killed. Why do you think so many chose to fight?

Jewish partisan activity

Despite enormous obstacles and incredible risks, historians suggest that between 20,000 and 30,000 Jews joined the **partisans**. Partisans were typically resistance groups who escaped capture by hiding in the forests of Eastern Europe (e.g. in Belarus, Lithuania, Poland and Ukraine). As the word cloud shows, they carried out many acts of resistance.

Destroyed bridges, train lines and roads
Stole and smuggled weapons
Worked with the Allies to defeat the Nazis
Forged identity papers
PARTISANS
Attacked the enemy
Smuggled food into ghettos
Helped escapes from camps and ghettos
Protected families

Figure 5.9 A group of partisans on the move in Ukraine.

The Bielski partisans

Three Jewish brothers, named Bielski, set up a partisan group in the Naliboki Forest in Belarus. The group fought against the Germans and their collaborators. They also protected families and built a thriving community which had a mill, a bakery, a school and a synagogue. Under the protection of the Bielski group, around 1,200 Jewish people survived the war.

Figure 5.10 Jews in the Bielski family camp in the Naliboki Forest, May 1944.

Activities

1 The Bielski partisans hid in the forest for almost five years. What dangers did they face? Why do you think 1,200 survived?

2 Hiding from the Nazis and their collaborators was also a form of resistance. A well-known example of this is the story of Anne Frank. Find out about Anne and her family and explain how they resisted the Nazis. What happened to them?

Jewish resistance across Europe

Armed resistance occurred in other parts of Europe too. For example, in France, the Armée Juive (Jewish Army) helped Jews escape from Nazi-occupied Europe and took part in uprisings against German troops in Paris and Lyon.

5.2 Who was responsible?

Why were six million Jewish people murdered during the Second World War? Many people would say because Hitler hated Jews, but Hitler was only one man who could never have killed millions of people alone. Explaining why and how the Holocaust happened is not easy or straightforward. But it is not impossible. A good place to start is by asking who did what, and thinking about the consequences that those actions had. This allows us to start to consider what people were responsible for. On the following pages, you will learn about the actions of just a few people.

Activities

1 Discuss the case studies in this chapter. For each one, note down what was done and what the consequences of these actions were.

2 How responsible (or not) were these people for the Holocaust? Use your notes from activity 1 and add to them.

Eleonore Gusenbauer

Gusenbauer's house overlooked a quarry where prisoners from Mauthausen concentration camp were forced to do hard physical labour. On 27 September 1941, she wrote a letter to the local police:

'Inmates … are constantly being shot … Those who are badly struck still live for some time and lie next to the dead for hours and in some cases for half a day. My property is situated on an elevation close [by] … and therefore one often becomes the unwilling witness of such misdeeds. I am sickly in any case and such sights make such demands on my nerves, that I will not be able to bear it much longer. I request that it be arranged that such inhuman deeds will cease or else be conducted out of sight.'

The 'Death Dealer'

On 23 June 1941, the German army occupied Kaunas in Lithuania. Two days later, Walter Stahlecker – the head of one of the *Einsatzgruppen* – visited the city. He gave antisemitic speeches and encouraged violence towards Jews living in Kaunas. People quickly followed his lead, and over the next four days, around 3,800 Jews were murdered. One of the worst events took place on the forecourt of a garage. Jews were dragged onto the yard where they were beaten to death by local civilians. One of these men was known as the 'Death Dealer'. Armed with a huge iron bar, he smashed people's skulls open as a watching crowd clapped and cheered.

Buying and selling possessions

When Jewish people were deported from Western Europe, they were only permitted to take a few belongings with them. The homes and possessions they were forced to leave behind were then offered to their neighbours to buy at discounted prices. On most occasions, the victims of the 'Holocaust by bullets' in Eastern Europe were told they were going to be moved elsewhere, and so were allowed to take some possessions. These belongings were seized, together with the victims' clothes. Sometimes the possessions were distributed or sold to the local population; at other times, they were sent back to Germany to be given away or sold there.

A Lithuanian policeman, returning from a mass shooting, sells property owned by Jewish people, July/August 1941.

The Trawniki men

In the village of Trawniki, in German-occupied Poland, there was a special camp. From September 1941 to summer 1944, around 5,000 Soviet prisoners of war were sent there for training. Most came from Ukraine, Latvia, or Lithuania. They were offered the chance to avoid starvation and disease in prisoner of war camps, in exchange for working for the Germans. From autumn 1942, civilians were also recruited from occupied countries. After training, the Trawniki men worked in the death camps and helped with **deportations** from ghettos. The men shown here are at Belzec in 1942.

René Bousquet

In the 1930s, Bousquet became a significant figure in French politics. In 1942, he became the Chief of Police. As part of the deals he made with the Germans, Bousquet became involved in the deportation of Jews from France. For example, over two days in summer 1942, Bousquet ordered the French police to arrest around 12,000 Jewish men, women and children in Paris. They were sent to a transit camp before being taken to Auschwitz. Later, in January 1943, Bousquet worked with the Germans to round up and deport over 2,000 Jews to camps in the East.

René Bousquet, on the right, smiling (23 January 1943).

Gertrude Segel

Segel was a typist for the Gestapo in Vienna. In early 1941, she volunteered to work for the security police in German-occupied Poland. There she began a relationship with an SS commander, Felix Landau. Segel joined Landau after he was sent to Ukraine. They lived in a stolen house with stolen goods, and had a balcony where they used to sit and watch Jewish workers in their garden. One day, either Segel or Landau shot one of the workers dead from the balcony. Another time, they wrongly accused a Jewish man of stealing a necklace from Segel. When he denied it, Landau beat him as Segel watched on.

Adolf Hitler

Adolf Hitler was obsessed with Jewish people and was intensely antisemitic. Hitler constantly blamed Jewish people for Germany's problems, and claimed Jews around the world threatened the survival of the 'Aryan race'. As the leader of Nazi Germany, he was in a position to spread his hatred of Jews. He did so in different ways. Sometimes he gave orders which directly impacted Jewish people. At other times people around him would try to guess what Hitler wanted and introduce new, more severe measures that targeted Jews. In both cases, he was always fully aware of what was happening to Europe's Jews.

Otto Julius Schimke

To keep order in territories conquered by Nazi Germany, regular German policemen were given military training, grouped into battalions, then sent to the East. There, they became involved in guarding ghettos and deporting people to death camps. On 13 July 1942, Police Battalion 101 arrived outside the Polish village of Józefów. For the first time, their commander Major Trapp told them to round up all Jewish women, children and elderly people in the village, take them to the forest and shoot them. Trapp said anyone who could not do this would be given other duties. Out of 486 men, only twelve stepped forward to opt out, including Schimke. He and the other eleven men did not shoot anyone in

Members of Battalion 101 celebrate Christmas, 1940.

Józefów. Instead, they guarded Jewish people as they were assembled in the village square. Schimke did not take part in other shootings either. He was part of the Battalion's other task: killing partisans (see page 71).

I.G. Farben

I.G. Farben was a collection of companies that specialised in chemicals. They became very important to the Nazis during the Second World War. In spring 1941, the Nazis allowed the company to construct a large industrial centre in Poland, seven kilometres from Auschwitz. Prisoners from Auschwitz were used as slave labour to build a large factory. I.G. Farben then paid the SS a discounted rate for these prisoners to work at the complex. In 1942, a camp named Auschwitz-Monowitz III was constructed next to the factory to house prisoners. Around 30,000 people died there due to lack of food and harsh working conditions.

I.G. Farben factory under construction, 1942.

Workers at the German census bureau

In May 1939, each household in Greater Germany had to complete a form with the names, ages, jobs, religion and 'race' of everyone who lived in their house. This data was then sorted by thousands of office workers. Using the forms, they would punch holes into cards to record the information. These cards were then fed through an early type of computer to create a register. This process of registration was repeated as Germany invaded other countries. The information helped the Nazis find and identify people they wanted to round up, deport, and even murder.

Henryk Gawkowski

During the Holocaust, millions of people were transported across huge distances to camps and ghettos. This required enormous planning and co-ordination across Europe's railway networks. Gawkowski lived close to Treblinka. When he was in his early twenties, he worked for a German-run railway company. Between 1942 and 1943, Gawkowski drove trains two or three times a week from cities in German-occupied Poland to Treblinka. He was paid and given vodka as a bonus, which he drank to cope with the smell. Altogether, he estimated taking

Gawkowski recreates driving a train to Treblinka for the documentary, *Shoah*, 1985.

around 18,000 Jews to the camp. After the war, because he knew what happened to the people he helped transport, 'it became very difficult for him'. Gawkowski had nightmares for the rest of his life.

5.3 Did anyone try to save the Jews?

The behaviour of non-Jews during the Holocaust varied greatly. The majority of people in Europe did nothing while Jews were rounded up and taken away. Some felt too afraid to do anything. Some wanted to protect their families by staying out of the way. Others did not care about what was happening to Jews and yet others agreed with their persecution. Many collaborated with the Nazis or led their own attacks against Jews. Others benefited from the property of their Jewish neighbours.

Nevertheless, there were some people who chose to help Jews. Some took great risks to do so. Rescue took many forms: some provided food or shelter to Jews, others gave them fake identity documents, and others helped Jews to hide or escape. Most rescue efforts were by groups or organisations, and involved networks of people.

Why did some people rescue Jews when others did not?

When thinking about why some people rescued Jews and others did not, it is important to remember that conditions in different parts of Europe varied. The Nazis, for example, were much more cruel and unforgiving towards the Polish than towards the Danes. We should also remember that different people think and act in different ways for different reasons. Rescuers were typically people who had a history of helping those in

need and who acted according to their beliefs, not caring what other people thought. Most rescuers did not plan to rescue but did so when presented with the choice.

In the next few pages, you will read some stories of rescue. These are not the only ones – many such stories exist and rescuers came from every country across Europe.

Think about

Rescuers took great risks to save Jews. However, Nechama Tec, a Holocaust scholar, found that most rescuers did not think their acts were heroic. Why do you think that is?

Case study: Denmark

Germany occupied Denmark in 1940 (see page 45). From the beginning of the Nazi occupation, the Danish government protected Jewish Danes from **discrimination**. In October 1943, the Danes refused to obey German orders to round up and deport Jews from Denmark. Instead, they organised a rescue operation. They helped Jews go into hiding and secretly reach the coast. From there, fishermen ferried them to neutral Sweden, which had agreed to receive them (see Figure 5.11). The Danish resistance, the police, the government and ordinary people took part in the rescue operation. In little more than three weeks, the Danes ferried more than 7,000 Jews to Sweden. They saved more than 95 per cent of Denmark's Jewish population.

The Thomsens

Henry Christian Thomsen and his wife Ellen Margrethe were innkeepers in the village of Snekkersten in Denmark. They were active members of the resistance. They sheltered fleeing Jews in their inn until the fishermen could take them to Sweden. Many villagers, including the local police, helped them. Henry even personally took Jews to Sweden by boat to help them escape. Henry was arrested by the Gestapo in August 1944 and sent to Neuengamme concentration camp in Germany. He died there four months later.

Source 5.1

… the lawless action of the Germans against the Jews was [seen] as an unnecessary German provocation against the core values of the Danish nation. It was judged 'un-Danish' because the Jews were considered an integral part of the Danish nation.

Karl Christian Lammers, Holocaust scholar

Activities

1 What does Source 5.1 tell you about why the Danes rescued Jews?
2 Try to find out more about why the Danes rescued Jews and what conditions made the rescues possible.

Figure 5.11 Jewish refugees are ferried out of Denmark aboard Danish fishing boats bound for Sweden.

Case study: Albania

In 1939, Albania was occupied by Germany's ally, Italy. The Italian fascist government enacted antisemitic policies but did not deport Jews to death camps. In 1943, Italy surrendered to the **Allied powers**, but German troops occupied the north of Italy and took over Albania too. From 1943 until 1945, approximately 8,000 Jews from Italy were deported to the death camps by the Nazis. However, in Albania, the Nazis encountered more resistance.

When they demanded that the Albanian authorities hand over all Jews in the country for deportation, the Albanian authorities refused. They provided many Jewish families with fake identity documents. Many Albanians hid Jewish families in their homes. They protected Jewish **refugees** who had arrived from other parts of Europe, as well as Albanian citizens. By the end of the war, Albania had saved the 2,000 Jews living within its borders.

The Veselis

Moshe and Ela Mandil and their children, Gavra and Irena, were a Jewish family who lived in Yugoslavia. When the Germans invaded Yugoslavia in April 1941, the family fled to Kosovo and then to Albania. Moshe found a job in an old friend's photography shop, where he met 17-year-old Refik Veseli. After the German invasion of Albania, Veseli took the Mandil family to his parents' home in the mountains. In Kruja, the Veselis provided shelter for the Mandils for nine months until the **liberation** of Albania.

Gavra Mandil and Refik Veseli in Tirana, 1944.

Source 5.2

When my husband was asked how it was possible that so many Albanians helped to hide Jews and protect them, he said: 'There are no foreigners in Albania, there are only guests.' Our moral code as Albanians requires that we be hospitable to guests in our home and in our country.

Drita Veseli, the wife of Refik Veseli

Activities

1 What does Source 5.2 tell you about why the Albanian people protected and rescued Jews?

2 The Albanian moral code that Drita is talking about in Source 5.2 is called 'Besa'. Try to find out more about it.

'Righteous Among the Nations'

Denmark and Albania are two examples of collective efforts to rescue Jews. Elsewhere in Europe, there were non-Jewish people who helped Jews. These individuals are recognised by the state of **Israel** and are given the honorary title of 'Righteous Among the Nations'. Today, 27,362 people from all over the world are recognised as Righteous.

Irena Sendler

Irena was a Polish social worker. When the Warsaw ghetto was created, she managed to get a permit that allowed her to enter the ghetto to inspect the conditions. She smuggled in food and medicines. She also smuggled out Jewish children and set up hiding places for them. In October 1943, she was arrested, interrogated and tortured, but she did not give up the addresses of the children in hiding. She was sentenced to death but the Polish resistance bribed the officials to release her. After her release, she continued her activities. She and her partners rescued about 2,500 children.

Chiune Sugihara

Chiune-Sempo Sugihara was a Japanese diplomat in Lithuania. In the summer of 1940, Lithuania was annexed by the Soviet Union and all foreign diplomats were asked to depart. As he was preparing to leave, a group of Jewish representatives asked to see him. They were desperate to escape, but they had nowhere to go. All the countries in the world had closed their borders. The refugees had learnt that Curaçao – in the Caribbean – did not require entry visas. All they needed to get there were visas that would allow them to travel eastwards. Sugihara was told not to issue the visas. Nevertheless, he provided 2,100–3,500 transit visas. The Jews who received them made a narrow escape from the *Einsatzgruppen*, who arrived in 1941. When Sugihara returned to Japan, he was fired and had to support his family by doing odd jobs.

Activities

1 What choices did Irena have at the beginning of her story? What choices did she have when she was arrested? What did she decide to do in each case? What were the risks Irena took and why do you think she decided to take them?

2 Why do you think Chiune decided to disobey his orders and issue the visas? What were the consequences of his choice?

Think about

Many people disagreed with what was happening to Jews. However, they decided not to intervene to help them, usually out of fear for their own and their family's safety. Do you think those people are to some degree responsible for what happened to Jews? Explain your thinking.

5.4 How did the British government respond to the Holocaust?

Some people wrongly believe that the British government didn't know about the persecution and murder of European Jews, or that Britain went to war with Nazi Germany to save the Jews of Europe. Neither of these is true. Most historians agree that:

- Britain declared war on Nazi Germany because Germany invaded Poland in September 1939.

- British decision-makers had knowledge of mass murder in the Soviet Union and the mass murder of Jews, in particular, as early as July 1941.

- In summer 1941, the war was not going well for Britain. There was very little they could have done to help the Jews of Europe.

- The British government repeatedly said that the best way to help the Jews of Europe was to defeat Nazi Germany and win the war.

- The British government said that they would punish the killers when the war was over.

Activities

Sort the information in the timeline below into two categories: knowledge and response. Some may fall into both.

1 What knowledge did the British government have about the persecution and mass murder of the Jews of Europe?

2 How did they respond to this knowledge?

What did the British government know and how did they respond?

Key events

November 1938 Following *Kristallnacht* (see page 40), relief organisations asked the British government to allow German and Austrian Jews into Britain. In total, approximately 80,000 Jewish refugees came to Britain. This was just a fraction of those in need.

December 1938 The first Kindertransport arrived in Britain. This scheme led to a total of 10,000 Jewish children coming to Britain from Nazi-controlled countries (see page 82).

May 1939 Some Jews wanted to go to Palestine (much of the region is known as Israel today). This is where Judaism began and where the holiest place is for Jews. Palestine was controlled by the British (the **British Mandate of Palestine**). To prevent unrest among the Arab population there, the British government introduced severe restrictions upon Jewish immigration into the British Mandate of Palestine. These restrictions were not relaxed during or after the war.

1940 In early 1940, the war was going badly for Britain. There was increasing anti-foreign feeling in Britain, in part fuelled by the press. In this atmosphere the government imprisoned thousands of Germans and Austrians, including 27,000 Jewish refugees. Most were released later that year but the experience was a traumatic one for many.

July–August 1941 German radio messages were decoded at Bletchley Park. They gave details of the numbers of people, including Jews, being shot by police and SS troops as they advanced into the Soviet Union. The British Prime Minister, Churchill, received summaries of this information in daily reports.

24 August 1941 Britain's Prime Minister Winston Churchill made a speech which was broadcast by the BBC. He referred to the actions of German police units in the Soviet Union and said 'We are in the presence of a crime without a name.'

Possible responses

There is an ongoing debate among historians about what Britain could have done to help Jews. Here are four examples:

- *Bomb the train lines to Auschwitz*. Until 1943, the British planes were out of range. From May 1944, with the capture of Italian airfields, British planes were within range to bomb Auschwitz. This action could have disrupted and delayed the murder of Hungary's Jews in 1944 (see page 62).

- *Allow more refugees into Britain and the British Mandate of Palestine*. In the 1930s, the British government worried that increasing numbers of refugees would be unpopular. If they allowed more into the British Mandate of Palestine, they feared that it would lead to Arab support for Nazi Germany. But this action would have allowed more Jewish people to reach safety.

- *Assist Jewish groups working in Nazi-occupied Europe*. Britain could have sent money to help underground Jewish organisations working in occupied Europe. This action would have helped Jews in hiding and those trying to resist the Nazis, thereby helping more Jews survive.

- *Offer support for Jews managing to escape*. Britain could have offered to support any Jewish refugees who escaped to neutral countries, such as Sweden and Switzerland. This action would have allowed more Jewish people to reach safety.

Think about

From these options, what, if anything, do you think Britain should have done?

June 1942 The *Daily Telegraph* published information that 700,000 Polish Jews had been murdered, naming Chelmno as one of the killing sites (see Chapter 4). The information came to Britain via the Polish Resistance.

August 1942 The British Foreign Office received a report which became known as the *Riegner Telegram*. This informed the British government that the Nazis had a plan to kill millions of European Jews.

17 December 1942 With increasing knowledge about the murder of Jews in Europe, the Government felt that it needed to act. Anthony Eden, the British Foreign Secretary, read out a statement in Parliament called the 'Joint Declaration by Members of the United Nations' on behalf of both the British and American governments. The statement ended with a pledge that those responsible for these crimes would be punished.

April 1943 The Bermuda Conference was held between Britain and the USA to discuss possible rescue plans for victims of the Nazis and to make plans for refugees. The conference achieved very little. Not one Jewish person was saved as a result of it.

June 1944 The British and the Americans received detailed reports about Auschwitz-Birkenau known as the Auschwitz protocols. They contained detailed information about the gas chambers and crematoria, based upon information from four men who had escaped from Auschwitz-Birkenau. Some argued that the train lines to Auschwitz-Birkenau should be bombed. It was decided that it was best to focus on winning the war.

15 April 1945 British troops discover the concentration camp of Bergen-Belsen. The discovery of Belsen came as a terrible shock to the liberating British troops (see page 65). Details of the conditions there were broadcast to the British public via radio, film and newspaper reports.

After the war the British government refused to allow mass immigration of Jewish survivors. Some were able to enter Britain as relatives of Jews already living in Britain. These refugees had to be supported by their families.

Case studies

Before the war: Jewish refugees and the *Kindertransport*

The *Kindertransport* scheme was organised by refugee aid committees, not the British government. Payment had to be guaranteed for the care of each child. They were supposed to go home when the crisis was over. Parents were not allowed to accompany their children. Many of the children never saw their parents again and were traumatised by their experience. Despite these challenges, the scheme saved the lives of approximately 10,000 children.

A Jewish girl, wearing a numbered tag, after her arrival in England with the second *Kindertransport*.

Internment: Bernd Simon

Bernd Simon had escaped Nazi Germany in 1933 with students and teachers from his school. His mother, Gerty Simon, a well-known photographer (see page 18), had followed her son to Britain. Despite having come to Britain as refugees, male teachers and students over the age of 16 from Bernd's former school were **interned** in 1940 (see timeline on page 80). Bernd, along with 2,500 other young men, most of whom were Jewish, were sent to Australia by ship. When they arrived there, they were interned in a camp. Bernd's release was finally agreed in late December 1941. Back in Britain, he worked to help the war effort until the end of the war.

After the war: 'The Boys'

The Committee for the Care of Children from Concentration Camps persuaded the British government to accept 1,000 Jewish children as refugees on condition that Britain's Jewish community would pay for them. In total, 732 children came to Britain, and though 80 of them were girls, they were given the nickname 'The Boys'. The first group of 300 were sent to Windermere in the Lake District with subsequent groups being placed in other locations across Britain. Many of 'the Boys' stayed in Britain and had happy and successful lives.

Four of 'The Boys', Jewish orphans brought to the UK as refugees after the war.

Think about

What more can we learn about British government responses from these case studies?

Different interpretations of Britain's response to the Holocaust

Many historians and politicians have tried to assess the response of the British government to the Holocaust. They have not always agreed. In fact, different interpretations of the actions of the British government exist. In the boxes below are examples of three different interpretations.

Interpretation 1

'I believe this period defines Britain and what it means to be British. It is Britain's unique response to the Holocaust and its unique role in the war that gives us the right to claim a particular attachment to the values of democracy, equality, freedom, fairness and tolerance.'

From Britain's Promise to Remember: The Prime Minister's Holocaust Commission Report

Interpretation 2

'There is little to celebrate in this account of British policy towards the Jews of Europe between 1939 and 1945 … The overall record leaves a profoundly saddening impression.'

Bernard Wasserstein, Britain and the Jews of Europe 1939–45

Interpretation 3

'In the summer of 1941 … the British could have done nothing, even if they had wanted to, to save European Jews from annihilation, but clearly they didn't want to. They could have done important things on the margins… Practically speaking, their options were limited, as was their realisation of what was going on.'

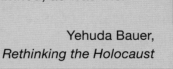

Yehuda Bauer,
Rethinking the Holocaust

Activity

Having considered the evidence on these pages, which of the three interpretations on this page do you consider best reflects Britain's response to the Holocaust? Explain your choice.

Now you have studied this unit, check your knowledge here:
www.ucl.ac.uk/holocaust-education

Develop knowledge and understanding

To deepen your knowledge and challenge common misunderstandings, you will learn:

- How Jewish communities across Europe were devastated by the Holocaust and that most were lost forever.
- About how other groups were victims of the Nazis and their **collaborators**.
- That many survivors continued to face difficulties after the end of the war.
- That **antisemitism** did not end with the defeat of the Nazis.
- That many survivors **emigrated** to other countries after the war, including **Israel** and Britain.
- How Jewish survivors were not always welcomed in other countries after the Holocaust.
- That 99 per cent of those who were responsible for the Holocaust never faced justice and were not punished.

Think historically

Interpretations of significance

There are many different ideas or interpretations about why the Holocaust is significant. Some are listed below. Pick three you agree most strongly with and explain why you chose them.

The Holocaust is significant because:

- it affected millions of lives
- it affected people deeply
- it affected people for a long time and still affects people today
- it develops our understanding of being human
- it teaches us where intolerance, racism and antisemitism can lead
- it shows human beings are capable of evil
- it teaches us not to be bystanders
- it teaches us that we all have a responsibility to improve our world
- it shows how fragile European civilisation is.

Discuss

- Did the Holocaust really end in 1945?
- Was justice done?
- What is the meaning of the Holocaust for you?

6.1 What was lost?

During the Holocaust, six million Jews were murdered, including one and a half million children – 90 per cent of all Jewish children living in Europe. The loss was devastating. Entire families, entire communities, entire towns and villages all across Europe no longer existed. Hopes and dreams were shattered, ways of life were destroyed, and the diversity of Jewish life and culture that existed before the war was gone forever. Before the Second World War, cities like Warsaw, Budapest and Vienna were bustling with Jewish life. Today, you can walk the streets of these cities and not meet a single Jewish person. Think of the huge void that was left by the loss of six million people, the families they never had, and the contributions to art, culture and science they were never able to make.

Figure 6.1 Children of the Jewish school in the *shtetl* Trochenbrod (in Ukraine) in 1934/35. In 1930, approximately 5,000 Jews lived in this town, which had seven synagogues and a rich farming culture.

Figure 6.2 The location of the Jewish *shtetl* Trochenbrod as it is today. During the Holocaust, the town's people, buildings and streets were completely destroyed.

Figure 6.3 The Jewish Museum, Berlin. The architect of this building (Daniel Libeskind) created these empty spaces, called 'voids'. They are meant to show the emptiness that resulted from the destruction of Jewish life in the Holocaust. He wanted to make this loss visible through architecture.

Activities

1 Look back at the map on pages 8–9. Which countries had the greatest Jewish losses? Which country did the largest number of Jewish people killed come from?

2 Look at Figures 6.1 and 6.2. What is the difference between these images? What do they tell us about the Holocaust?

3 Look at Figure 6.3. How did the architect of the Jewish Museum in Berlin try to show the void that was created by the Holocaust? Undertake some research on other ways people have tried to express this huge loss.

Other victims of the Nazis

The Nazis **persecuted** other groups, as well as Jews. Estimates of how many were killed are based on census reports, Nazi documents and post-war investigations.

Activity

Read the information on this page. Undertake further research into the suffering of one of these groups at the hands of the Nazis.

Soviet civilians and prisoners of war (POWs)

Soviet prisoners of war (POWs) were killed by the Nazis on a mass scale. Out of approximately 5.7 million Soviet prisoners, 3.3 million were murdered. In addition, millions of Soviet civilians were starved or worked to death. The Nazis also brutally murdered vast numbers of Soviet civilians at any sign of opposition or resistance.

Political opponents

In 1933, the Nazis established concentration camps to imprison German **political opponents** (see page 27). They were treated brutally but most were released. During the war, as the German soldiers advanced to the east, they were given orders to shoot and kill all **Communist** Party officials they could find. The killing included anyone who was perceived as a threat, such as intellectuals, priests and **partisans**.

Polish civilians

During the German invasion of Poland, many Polish civilians were shot, and many more were sent to **concentration camps**. Hundreds of thousands were forced to leave the west of Poland to make room for Germans. About 1.5 million Poles were used as slave labour. It is estimated that 1.8 million non-Jewish Polish civilians were killed during the Second World War.

Disabled people

During the war, the children's **'euthanasia' programme** murdered around 5,000 disabled children. The adult 'euthanasia' programme (see page 32) began killing by gas in the winter of 1939 and was officially halted in 1941, when more than 70,000 adults in Greater Germany and German-occupied Poland had been murdered. The programme secretly continued and approximately 250,000 disabled people were killed by the end of the war.

Roma and Sinti ('Gypsies')

When the Nazis came to power, they persecuted the **Roma and Sinti** within Greater Germany. Their racist laws were applied to the 'Gypsies'. Many were arrested without cause and many were forcibly sterilised. After the outbreak of war, Roma and Sinti were murdered in **death camps** and died of hunger and disease in forced labour and concentration camps. An estimated 500,000 people died. The **genocide** is sometimes referred to as *Pharrajimos* – the Great Devouring.

6.2 What was it like to survive the Holocaust?

Liberation

The Second World War ended in Europe on 8 May 1945. For those Jews who had survived, **liberation** was the start of a long journey. Jews had been living in fear for years; they were physically and mentally exhausted, starving, and suffering from diseases due to the terrible conditions in the camps. Now, they had to gather up the strength to face what had happened.

Source 6.1
That day ..., was the saddest day of my life. I wanted to cry, not from joy but from grief.

From the testimony of Yitzhak Zuckerman

Source 6.2
My bones stuck out from under my skin. All my joints were full of pus, my knees, my elbows, my throat ... They thought it was diphtheria; it wasn't ... it was the onset of death [...] And suddenly Lusia came and said 'The war is over.' I still remember the feeling. I thought 'Now? What for? It's no longer possible to live, there's nothing anymore. Where were they before? What's the use of it now?'

From the testimony of Miriam Akavia

Activities

1 Why do you think Yitzhak felt so sad on the day of his liberation?

2 How would you describe Miriam's feelings on the day of liberation?

Figure 6.4 A survivor sitting alone after his liberation at Bergen-Belsen, April 1945.

Facing what happened

As soon as they could, survivors began to look for their family. They looked in the registers of survivors in camps, contacted the Red Cross or returned home to see what was left. Most were not successful. The vast majority of survivors were the only survivors of their entire family.

Those who decided to return home faced a harsh reality: they had no family left, no home, no community and no possessions. The places they remembered as 'home' before the war were no longer the same.

Source 6.3

Suddenly I am standing in the middle of the city [...] and I ask myself, 'So what? Home – gone, family – gone, children – gone, friends are gone, Jews – gone ... This is what I fought for? This is what I stayed alive for?' Suddenly I realised that my whole struggle had been pointless, and I didn't feel like living.

From the testimony of Shmuel Shulman Shilo

Starting over

Many survivors who returned to their homes – especially in Eastern and Central Europe – soon realised that they were not welcome by many local people. Indeed, after the war, on numerous occasions, some local populations carried out antisemitic attacks on survivors. The biggest **pogrom** took place in Kielce, Poland, where 42 Jewish survivors were murdered on 4 July 1946.

Source 6.4

I went home. I didn't have anywhere I could stay ... The gatekeeper was living in the house and wouldn't let me go in ... I had aunts and family. I went to see all their apartments. There were non-Jews living in every one. They wouldn't let me in. In one place, one of them said, 'What did you come back for? They took you away to kill you, so why did you have to come back?' I decided: I'm not staying here, I'm going.

From the testimony of Shoshana Stark

Figure 6.5 One of the young survivors of Buchenwald concentration camp writes in German 'Where are our parents?' on the side of a train leaving the camp.

Displaced persons camps

Because of this hostility, and because they had nothing left, many Jews decided to emigrate to another country. Emigration was not easy because countries were not allowing many **refugees** to enter. Until they could get visas to emigrate, hundreds of thousands of survivors lived in displaced persons camps (DP camps).

DP camps were created by the **Allied powers** in Germany, Austria and Italy. Life in the DP camps was difficult, but survivors slowly began to build their lives again.

Figure 6.6 A nursery school at Bindermichl DP camp, Austria.

Emigration

The USA, Canada and the UK were all potential destinations, but the majority of Jewish refugees wanted to emigrate to the **British Mandate of Palestine**. Between 1945 and 1948, around 70,000 survivors tried to emigrate there, but the British government, which ruled Palestine at the time, would not allow them to because they were concerned about Arab unrest in the region (see page 80). The British navy stopped ships carrying survivors and detained most of the refugees on Cyprus.

In 1947, the British handed control of the British Mandate of Palestine to the United Nations, which voted to separate the territory into two parts, one Arab and one Jewish. Although the Arabs objected, in May 1948 the state of Israel was declared. Significantly, every Jewish person who wanted to enter Israel could now do so. It is estimated that 170,000 Jewish people had immigrated to Israel by 1953.

Figure 6.7 The *Exodus 1947* with Jewish Holocaust survivors on board.

Activity

Look at Figure 6.7. Undertake some research into *Exodus 1947*. Find out about the boat's journey and what happened to the Jewish survivors on-board.

Holocaust survivors in Britain

After the war, the British government did not allow many survivors to emigrate to the United Kingdom. Some of those who came to Britain had relatives already living there – they supported survivors without government help. A number of survivors received emotional and financial support from non-governmental organisations.

While the British people were shocked to learn about what happened to Jews during the Holocaust, they were less interested in hearing the stories of the survivors. Their experiences were generally ignored.

Many survivors, in any case, found themselves unable to speak about what they witnessed and suffered. They were often very disturbed and traumatised by their experiences. They even found it difficult to talk to their own family. It was all too painful. Sometimes the impact of the Holocaust not only affected survivors but also their children.

Survivors faced other challenges. Many were tormented by horrific nightmares. Some struggled to trust other people and never felt completely safe again. Despite these difficulties, survivors were remarkably resilient. Typically, they led fulfilling lives, built homes, families and futures. They found jobs and worked hard. They contributed significantly to Britain in all manner of ways. Most survivors were not filled with feelings of revenge or bitterness. They often maintained a positive outlook on life.

Source 6.5
My uncle was at the quayside in Dover to meet us. His greeting was chilly: 'Welcome to England. Understand that in my house I don't want you to speak about anything that happened to you. I don't want to know and I don't want my girls upset.'

Kitty Hart-Moxon, a Holocaust survivor, describes the day she arrived in Britain.

Source 6.6
My father never spoke about the Holocaust until I was much older … [but] his traumatic experiences changed him. He saw invisible danger wherever he looked and did not really believe that safety existed. Like many other children [born] to Holocaust survivors, there was a huge gap between my actual safe surroundings and the traumatic environment of my father's mind. I grew up within this contradiction; trying to hold on to safety whilst breathing in invisible trauma that made me strangely hyper-vigilant, worried and unsafe.

From the testimony of the son of a Jewish survivor, North London

Activities
1 Read Source 6.5. Why do you think people may not have wanted to listen to survivors after the war? How do you think the experience Kitty describes made her feel as she began her life in Britain?
2 Read Source 6.6. How does the son of a survivor describe the impact of the Holocaust on him?

In more recent years, a number of survivors have felt able to talk about their experiences during the Holocaust. Many spend their retirement years travelling across Britain to meet teachers and students. They tell their harrowing stories as sensitively as they can, and they answer students' questions. Re-living the memory of the Holocaust is never easy and it often takes several hours for a survivor to fully recover from just one talk at a school or college.

Source 6.7

I must speak for those who were lost. I feel it is my duty to remember the many who otherwise will never be remembered. If I didn't it would be as if they never existed. I could never betray their memory.

Mala Tribich, a Holocaust survivor

Leon Greenman

After the war, Leon Greenman (see page 13) returned to London. He had lost everything. His wife and child were murdered at Auschwitz-Birkenau. Leon never remarried. He became a market trader in Petticoat Lane. In his eighties, he became an activist fighting racism through peaceful demonstration and education. It became his mission. He died at the age of 97 in 2008. By the end of his life he had given his **testimony** to hundreds of thousands of people.

Think about

Why do survivors put themselves through the painful experience of telling their story to young people? Sources 6.7 and 6.8 may help develop your thinking.

Source 6.8

Revenge does not bring back the dead.
Does not take away the suffering,
it simply perpetuates the violence.

It is difficult to get convictions,
the question is "not to let it happen again?"

I have tried to rebuild my life,
a new life???
I have no children, no grandchildren to cuddle.

Have I succeeded? I don't know,
being too busy with this work,
seems to be my mission??

A poem written by Leon Greenman. The poem was found by his close and trusted friend Ruth-Anne Lenga in his house after his death. She worked closely with Leon as he educated young people at the Jewish Museum in London and travelled around the country to talk to students in schools and colleges.

Activity

What does Leon's poem tell us about the long-term impact of the Holocaust on his life?

6.3 Was there justice?

Before the defeat of **Nazi Germany**, the wartime Allied powers agreed that there could be no negotiation with the Nazis and that defeated Germany would be divided into zones of military occupation (Soviet, British, French and American zones). They also agreed to destroy Nazi control and influence in Germany and punish those responsible for war crimes. This process was known as de-Nazification.

When the war ended, the Nazi party was banned and Nazi symbols were removed from public places across all the occupation zones. The first trial of war criminals was held in Nuremberg, Germany, in 1945–46. The judges came from Great Britain, France, the Soviet Union and the United States of America. Of the 22 defendants, 19 were convicted and 10 of them were sentenced to death.

Between 1946 and 1949, there were 12 more trials in Nuremberg with a total of 199 German government officials, military leaders, SS, doctors, lawyers and industrialists brought to justice. A total of 161 were convicted.

Think about

Do you agree with the Nuremberg judges that 'following orders' does not excuse murder?

The *Einsatzgruppen* trial (1947–48)

One of the trials that took place in Nuremberg was the trial of 24 leaders of the SS mobile killing units (see page 51). The defendants admitted the crimes, but claimed that they were not responsible because they were only following orders from their superiors. They pleaded 'not guilty', but the court found them guilty and sentenced some to death, and others to imprisonment. The judges at the Nuremberg trials did not accept 'following orders' as an adequate defence for criminal acts.

The defendants sit in the dock at the *Einsatzgruppen* trial.

Was justice done?

The Allied powers had a policy that all Germans held a moral responsibility for the crimes carried out by the Nazis and their collaborators. German civilians and soldiers were shown images and films of Nazi concentration camps (see Figure 6.8). German civilians who lived near concentration camps were forced to visit the sites to witness the conditions there. In some cases they were forced to bury bodies and to hand over some of their possessions to help former prisoners.

Soon, however, the Allied powers decided to hand responsibility for de-Nazification to the Germans themselves. The Germans carried out some more trials, but very few people were convicted. According to historian Mary Fulbrook, 99 per cent of people who killed Jews were never brought to trial. Many returned to their homes and families. Many others escaped to countries outside Europe. Typically, perpetrators and collaborators from across Europe were never made to face responsibility for their actions.

Figure 6.8 German prisoners of war, held in an American hospital, are forced to watch a film showing the terrible conditions in German concentration camps.

Source 6.9

The total number of persons convicted in the Federal Republic [of Germany] for Nazi crimes was in itself fewer even than the number employed at Auschwitz alone.

Mary Fulbrook, Holocaust scholar

Think about

Although rare, trials of Nazi criminals have occurred recently. For example, in 2019, an SS guard named Bruno Dey was tried for his crimes. When the trial started, he was 93 years old. Some people believe that people as old as Bruno Dey should not be put on trial after all these years. For the survivors, a trial like Bruno's is important. Why do you think these trials are important for them? What is your opinion on whether these trials should still take place?

Now you have studied this unit, check your knowledge here:
www.ucl.ac.uk/holocaust-education

Across the world, Holocaust museums, memorials and monuments have been built as sites of education and remembrance. For example, at the time of writing, in the United Kingdom a new Memorial and Learning Centre is planned to be built next to the Palace of Westminster in London. Deciding what to include in any museum, memorial or learning centre is a very important and difficult responsibility.

Activity

In a city near you, a new Holocaust Learning Centre has been proposed. You have been asked to advise the city council on what to include in it. In particular, you need to decide on three elements:

1 What key knowledge about the Holocaust should the Learning Centre include?

UCL research with secondary school students showed that many young people have limited knowledge about the Holocaust. This textbook identifies some of the essential knowledge students need to know to challenge common misunderstandings. Look again at the units and write down six key facts that you believe are important for all visitors to know when they visit the Learning Centre. These key facts will be displayed prominently in different spaces within the Centre. Next to each key fact, briefly explain why this information is important for people to know.

2 What photographs should the Learning Centre display in its entrance hall?

You have also been asked to identify three photographs that will be enlarged and displayed in the entrance hall to the Learning Centre. Look back through the book and choose three photographs you would like displayed. Write a paragraph for each one, explaining why you chose it.

3 Which individuals should feature on the walls of the Centre?

Throughout this book, you have read about the lives of many individuals who were affected by the Holocaust. Select three of these. Their stories will be displayed on the walls of the Learning Centre. Write a brief explanation of why you chose these three people. What information about their lives do you think is important for visitors to know about?

Glossary

A larger, printable version of this glossary can be found on the UCL Centre for Holocaust Education website: www.ucl.ac.uk/holocaust-education.

Allied powers: The countries that fought against Germany. These include Britain, France (except the period of Nazi occupation 1940–44), the Soviet Union from June 1941 and the USA from December 1941, but there were many other 'Allied' nations.

Allies: Countries which formally cooperate with each other for a military or other purpose.

Anschluss: A German word for 'union'. The word refers to the joining of Austria with Nazi Germany in March 1938.

Antisemitism: Hostility to or prejudice against Jews.

Assimilated: When someone becomes part of the wider society and culture.

Axis powers: Those countries which fought with Germany. These include Italy, Japan, Hungary, Romania, Bulgaria and other countries.

British Mandate of Palestine: After the defeat of the Ottoman Empire in the First World War, the League of Nations placed the Middle Eastern territory known as 'Palestine' under British control. It was referred to as the British Mandate of Palestine. The British ruled the area from 1920 until 1948.

Castrated: When an individual loses use of the testicles, either by surgical or chemical action. Causes the individual to become sterile (unable to have children).

Collaborators: People, organisations and governments that helped the Nazis persecute and/or murder Jews.

Communist: A person who supports and believes in the principles of communism. Communism is a political ideology about how societies and economies should be organised. It argues, for instance, that resources and industries be collectively owned for the benefit of everyone.

Compensation: Something, usually money, given to someone in recognition of loss, suffering, or injury.

Concentration camps: Places where large numbers of people were kept as prisoners under armed guard.

Curfew: A rule requiring people to leave the streets or be at home at a certain time.

Death camp: Killing centres established by the Nazis in Central Europe during the Second World War. There were six sites: Chelmno, Belzec, Sobibor, Treblinka, Majdanek, and Auschwitz-Birkenau. Approximately 2.5 million European Jews were murdered at these places primarily by gassing in specially built chambers or gas vans. Roma and Sinti and other victims were also murdered in the death camps.

Demonised: Something or someone portrayed as wicked and threatening.

Deportation: Forcibly removing someone from one country to another.

Dictator: A person who rules with total authority.

Discrimination: Unfairly treating an individual or a group differently from others.

Einsatzgruppen: special units of the Security Police and SD. With the help of the SS, police units, the army and local collaborators, the *Einsatzgruppen* conducted mass shootings in the Soviet Union, targeting Jews, Roma, communists and Soviet civilians.

Emigrate: To leave the country you live in to move to a different country. This movement might be voluntary, or it might be forced upon someone by war, conflict, or natural disaster.

Enabling Act: An act passed by the Reichstag (the German parliament) on 23 March 1933 which gave Hitler the right to make laws without the Reichstag's approval for the next four years. It gave Hitler and the Nazis absolute power to make laws, which enabled them to destroy all opposition.

'Euthanasia' programme: Euthanasia means literally 'good death'. It usually refers to causing a painless death for a seriously ill individual who would otherwise suffer. In the Nazi era, however, the term was used for a secret murder programme. Its goal was to kill people with mental and physical disabilities who, the Nazis believed, weakened the 'Aryan race'.

Expel: Force someone to leave a place.

Genocide: Any act committed with intent to destroy, in whole or in part, a national, ethnic, racial or religious group. In 1944, after witnessing Nazi brutality in occupied Europe, the Jewish-Polish lawyer Raphael Lemkin invented the phrase 'genocide'. The term combined the Greek word *genos* (race or tribe) with the Latin word *cide* (to kill). On December 9 1948 the United Nations declared genocide to be an international crime.

Ghettos: Areas in towns or cities where Jews were separated by force from other people. Ghettos were overcrowded and living conditions were miserable. The first recorded ghetto was created in Venice, Italy, in 1516.

Great Depression: The worst economic downturn in the history of the industrialised world. It started in 1929 in the USA but because Germany depended on American financial support it led to the collapse of the German economy.

Interned: Being confined as a prisoner, especially for political or military reasons.

Israel: A country between Jordan and the Mediterranean Sea. Established in 1948 as a Jewish state in a region that was formerly known as the British Mandate of Palestine. Many regard the land of Israel to be the ancient homeland of the Jewish people.

Jehovah's Witnesses: Christians who worship Jehovah, the God of the Bible. They have certain distinct beliefs. Many refused to serve in the army or accept the Nazi's total power, believing that they were first answerable to God.

Liberation: Setting someone free.

Nazi Germany: The German state between 1933 and 1945, when Adolf Hitler and the Nazi Party controlled the country.

Neutrality agreement: An agreement between countries not to take military action against each other. In August 1939, Germany and the Soviet Union signed a neutrality agreement known as the Molotov-Ribbentrop Pact or the Nazi-Soviet Pact.

Orthodox Jews: Jews who understand their religion – Judaism – in a traditional way and live their lives according to religious laws.

Partisan: a member of an armed group formed to fight against an occupying force.

Persecution/Persecuted: Being treated badly, usually because of 'race' or religious or political beliefs.

Pogrom: An organised massacre of a particular group.

Police state: A state controlled by a political police force that secretly supervises people's activities.

Political opponents: People who belong to a different party or who have different ideas and beliefs.

Prejudice: An unfair opinion, judgement or feeling towards someone.

Propaganda: Spreading information, which is often false or misleading, to persuade people to support a point of view or cause.

Rations: A fixed amount of food or other necessities (such as soap) that each person is allowed to have.

Refugees: People who have been forced out of their country and cannot return home safely.

Remilitarise: To militarise again; rearm after being disarmed. After the First World War, the Treaty of Versailles did not allow the German army in the Rhineland. In March 1936, however, Hitler ordered German troops to enter it.

'Resettlement': An expression often used by the Nazis to refer to the deportation of Jews and others to sites of murder located in Eastern Europe.

Roma and Sinti: Roma and Sinti are the largest European minority and have lived in Europe for over 1,000 years. 'Sinti' refers to the members of an ethnic minority that settled in Germany and neighbouring countries in the early fifteenth century. 'Roma' refers to the ethnic minority that has lived in Eastern and South-Eastern Europe since the Middle Ages. Some Roma migrated to Western Europe in the eighteenth century. Roma and Sinti is the real name of the so called 'Gypsies'.

Scapegoat: Someone who is blamed for the wrongdoings, mistakes or faults of others.

Shtetls: Towns or villages with a large Jewish population.

Sub camps: Concentration camps and work camps often had a network of smaller camps attached to them, known as sub camps.

Testimony: A spoken or written statement describing an event or experience.

Trade Union: An organised association of workers in a trade or profession, formed to protect and further their rights and interests.

Work camps: Camps in which prisoners were forced to work as slave labourers.

Yiddish: A form of German usually spoken by Jewish people in Eastern Europe at this time.